I'LL DROP YOU OFF

A 40-Day Devotional for Cowboys.

By Kris Wilson

This devotional is dedicated to all the men and women I have had the pleasure of working with. I hope this book blesses you as much as it did me.

I would also like to dedicate this devotional to my wife, Cara. You have been my rock. -Kris

Special thanks to Rachel Cutrer with Ranch House Designs for publishing and Ross Hecox with Western Horseman Magazine for editing this book.

Address editorial correspondence to:
Kris Wilson
706 Mule Creek Drive
Solano, NM 87746
krwilson00@gmail.com

Cover photo by Peter Robbins
Back cover photo by Ron Gill

Originally published July 2016
Copyright ©2016 by Kris Wilson

All rights reserved. No part of this publication may be reproduced or transmitted in any form or by any means, electronic or mechanical, including photocopy, recording, or any information storage or retrieval system, without permission in writing from the publisher.

Table of Contents

Day 1: "In His Image" 7
Day 2: "From the Wilderness" 9
Day 3: "Valorous" 11
Day 4: "Bold" 13
Day 5: "Reckless" 15
Day 6: "Dedicated" 17
Day 7: "Honorable" 19
Day 8: "Longing to be a Cowboy" 21
Day 9: "No Apology Needed" 23
Day 10: "Fighting For Your Heart" 25
Day 11: "Learning to Live" 27
Day 12: "Finding Your Eve" 29
Day 13: "Where Did It All Go Wrong" 31
Day 14: "The Spread of Sin In Man" 33
Day 15: "The Great Cover-Up" 35
Day 16: "Our Inadequacies" 37
Day 17: "The Vices of Men" 39
Day 18: "The Question that Haunts Us All" 41
Day 19: "Our Father and Our Biggest Scar" 43
Day 20: "You Are a Lost Sheep" 45
Day 21: "Church" 47
Day 22: "Let's Get Over Ourselves" 49
Day 23: "I Need You" 51
Day 24: "It Is Finished" 53
Day 25: "Who's Ridin' This Horse?" 57
Day 26: "For You Created Me" 61
Day 27: "Things Might Get Tough" 63
Day 28: "A Wordly Solution" 65
Day 29: "Gut Check" 67
Day 30: "Harden Your Hope" 69
Day 31: "Listen, Obey, and Rejoice" 71
Day 32: "His Promise to Fight For Us" 73
Day 33: "The Six Things That Really Matter" 75
Day 34: "In His Time" 79
Day 35: "The Thorn In My Side" 81
Day 36: "Your Greatest Test" 83
Day 37: "Look Around" 85
Day 38: "The Best Day of My Life" 87
Day 39: "Your Purpose" 89
Day 40: "I'll Drop You Off" 91

Introduction

I've read too many Christian books and devotionals that start with an apology for writing "another" Christian-based book or an apology because the author doesn't feel qualified to be writing the material. I'm not going to do either. The reason is because God told me to write this devotional. I've been in the middle of a trial for the last three years—one that has just about taken all of my physical person from me, but it has strengthened my faith and my hope beyond measure. It has been a journey that I didn't ask for, but one that I have learned to appreciate.

About a year ago, in the midst of losing hope, I pictured Jesus in a dream as a fiery being on a horse riding toward me over a hill. It was how I had always pictured Him in the following scripture: "I saw heaven standing open and there before me was a white horse, whose rider is called Faithful and True. With justice he judges and wages war. His eyes are like blazing fire, and on his head are many crowns. He has a name written on him that no one knows but he himself. He is dressed in a robe dipped in blood, and his name is the Word of God." (Revelation 19:11-13 NIV). I bet some of you are about to stop reading. Another whacko, right? Hang with me for a minute. That scripture had always had a profound influence on me because of the detail by which He, our Lord Almighty, is described, and of course, my fascination with horses. The Lord used that visual to bring me a message. When I first saw the rider, I was frightened, but I quickly became relieved. I had been through so much pain and disappointment that for a moment I hoped that He was coming for me. However, His intentions were quickly revealed to me. Just like I had always imagined from the scriptures, His voice trumpeted very loudly and said, "I am not finished with you. I have plans for your works."

Over the next few days and weeks, the Lord revealed to me that the reason He was not finished with me was that He wanted me to write a devotional. He wanted me to write a devotional for cowboys. You see, working cowboys are an independent, self-reliant bunch. And while a great many are devoted Christians, there are many more to reach. What better way to reach a group of working cowboys than to reach them through one of their own? For cowboys there is a set of unwritten rules known as cowboy etiquette. Not all the rules are the same, and often they will be different from outfit to outfit. However, one thing remains the same. The rules are deeply rooted in a respect for one another, the animals they work with and the quality by which they perform their job or trade. Respect amongst a group of men or cowboys is earned and not bestowed. I have been blessed to spend the last twenty years as a horseman. I have shown, judged shows and conducted clinics in many states and several foreign countries. However, I have also been blessed to spend the last 7 years as a working cowboy. I have had the opportunity to work for a few of the most respected and iconic ranches in the WEST and have worked my way from cowboy to general manager.

Because of the nature of their work, cowboys are a busy group. They generally don't have a lot of time to sit and read. For this devotional, all I'm asking is for a few minutes a day for 40 days. "Why 40 days," you ask? Throughout the Bible, God did some miraculous things in people's lives in 40 days. In the Old Testament, after God told Noah to build a boat, He destroyed the world with water by making it rain 40 days and 40 nights (Genesis 7:12). God dealt with Moses in units of 40 on three different occasions—once in the desert for 40 years (Acts 7:30), on Mount Sinai for 40 days and 40 nights (Exodus 24:18) and for 40 days Moses interceded on Israel's behalf (Deuteronomy 9:18, 25). Goliath taunted Saul's army for 40 days before David took up his slingshot (1 Samuel 17:16). In the New Testament, Jesus was tempted in the desert for 40 days and 40 nights (Matthew 4:2), and there were 40 days between His resurrection and ascension into heaven (Acts 1:3). So, as you can see, God can do some miraculous things in the lives of people in 40 days. From building up the gumption of David to slay a giant, to building up the resolve in His own Son to bring the Message to His people. In the next 40 days, the Lord wants to do the same to you. He wants to transform you from a cowboy to a Christian. He wants to transform you from a man to a blood-bought, born-again child of the Most High God.

All of our walks are different. You may not know a thing about Jesus, but that's okay, just give Him 40 days. Or, you may be the pastor of a cowboy church, that's okay, just give Him 40 days. God wants to transform our hearts and our minds in the next 40 days. He wants to show you your very own burning bush, give you the courage of David, and prepare you like His church in the book of Acts. All He is asking for is a few minutes a day for the next 40 days.

When we trot out in the morning, headed out for a big drive or a gather through a pasture, whoever the boss is leads the way. Now the boss isn't necessarily the manager or the foreman, but the boss is the person who takes care of the cattle and the country that we are working in that day. He knows the country best, knows the cattle and knows where they have been grazing. He knows where they usually like to hang up, and knows how he wants to best work them that day. So, everyone else in the crew looks to him with their undivided attention. That's the etiquette or respect I mentioned earlier. The boss assigns responsibilities and demands total control of the works that day. One of the most important duties that he will perform that day is drop each cowboy in a specific spot before beginning the drive. When he trots out, everyone jigs in behind him in an orderly fashion and remains in that exact order. One-by-one he assigns each cowboy to a position. When he tells you to drop off, the location where he leaves you is critical, as it is the "country" that you will ride and gather that morning. Together, with a cowboy on each side (sometimes over half a mile away), you will methodically weave and work your way over the terrain gathering the stock to the predetermined "hold up." Most of the time it works seamlessly because of the control of the boss and the respect and willingness of his crew.

For the next 40 days, let Him drop you off. Try it. Give God the same undivided attention that you give your drive leader every morning. In the next 40 days, He has a plan to change your life. "'For I know the plans I have for you,' declares the Lord, 'plans to prosper you and not to harm you, plans to give you hope and a future. Then you will call on me and come and pray to me, and I will listen to you. You will seek me and find me when you seek me with all your heart" (Jeremiah 29:11-13 NIV).

Whether you are a working cowboy on a line camp somewhere, or a weekend warrior who simply loves the lifestyle, give Him the opportunity to move in your life. You may not be the cowboy yourself. You may be his wife, mother, father, brother, sister or friend. That's okay, give Him the opportunity to move in your life. You may not be a cowboy at all simply because you are a cowgirl. That's okay, one of my best full-time cowboys is a cowgirl. If that's you, give Him the opportunity to move in your life. For the next 40 days, pull your cinch tight, jig in behind Christ, give Him your undivided attention, and allow Him to drop you off.

Unit 1
Who We Are

Day 1
"In His Image"

"So God created mankind in His own image, in the image of God He created them; male and female He created them" (Genesis 1:27 NIV).

If you aren't ready to get real for the next 40 days, then I suggest you conveniently leave this devotional in the bunkhouse for someone else to pick up. Or, maybe you can opportunely leave it in your neighbor's feed pickup. Either way, that will be fine because I'm going to expose myself and God. I am going to expose our cowboy culture, and if you are breathing you will be exposed as well. If you are ready to quit playing "life," then saddle up. Basically it's time for us to get real.

Why don't we see more cowboys in church? Why don't we see more cowboys acting like men and leading their household in prayer like God instructed? Why don't we hear about cowboys witnessing to others and living boldly for Christ? "I'm busy," you say. "You know I've got those heifers to check, and that windmill in the Salt Creek pasture has been giving me heck." Fair enough. Not really, but fair enough. So if you don't' have time to devote your life to Christ, are you content to let your best friends perish? Ready to get real?

So, maybe you were raised in a church-going household, your mother was a fervent follower of Christ, and you were baptized. You know the Lord, but have never shared Him with anyone. You have the tools to fix things, but you watch as your non-believing friends perish. "Well, it's not my place to get in his business," you respond. Maybe not, but, "For the wages of sin is death, but the gift of God is eternal life in Christ Jesus our Lord" (Romans 6:23 NIV). So, you like him enough to go roping with him every Thursday evening, but you don't think enough of him to see him not perish? Some kind of man.

"I can't relate with those men at church," one friend told me. Know what? I don't blame him. Who wants to be like the man who wears the sweater vest who sits on the second pew to the right of the pulpit every week? Every week he's there, being dutiful. He doesn't say anything until after church when he catches you. You tried to slip out, but he says, "Sure glad you could join us this week. Why don't you join us for next Wednesday's prayer breakfast?" The nerve of that guy. Doesn't he realize that I've got a job to do? I mean it's branding time. I'm lucky I could slip over here on a Sunday. I've got things to do. All he has to do is decide which sweater he is going to wear that day. Know what? I understand. We are cowboys, right? We have cattle and horses to take care of; we have things to do. We are bold, and we only take instruction from men we respect. But, it's not his fault. He is doing what he thinks is right. The problem is that society has corrupted our relationship with God. Church-going men aren't supposed to be bold society has told us. Church going men are supposed to be meek, mild and subdued. So shut up and go find your favorite sweater vest!

The problem with that narrative is that it's not true at all. Our God is that same God who parted the waters of the Red Sea and drowned the whole Egyptian army (Exodus 14:21-23), the same God who picked up a whip made of cords and drove everyone from His temple (John 2:15), and the same God who defeated Satan. "He replied, 'I saw Satan fall like lightning from heaven. I have given you authority to trample on snakes and scorpions and to overcome all the power of the enemy; nothing will harm you" (Luke 10:18-19 NIV). Our God is a God of valiant men, and we have been created in His image. So, there is no need to apologize for being bold. There is no need to apologize for being audacious or courageous. There is no need to apologize for being a man and there is certainly no need to apologize for being a cowboy.

Day 2
"From the Wilderness"

"Then the Lord God formed a man from the dust of the ground and breathed into his nostrils the breath of life, and the man became a living being. Now the Lord God had planted a garden in the east, in Eden; and there he put the man he had formed" (Genesis 2:7-8 NIV).

In his book *Wild at Heart*, John Eldredge pointed out that man was not created in the Garden of Eden. In the above passage it says that God breathed life into man first, and then God put man into the newly planted garden. If you think about that for a minute, it makes sense why men are drawn to the wild. When I came to the Bell Ranch as manager, it was my goal for the ranch to pull a wagon again. The practice of pulling a wooden wheeled wagon by a team of horses during branding season had been abandoned by the Bell in the late 1950s. Up until five or six years before I arrived, the ranch still used a "wagon crew" in the spring, but they had recently abandoned the practice altogether. To me, if we could do our works as effectively and efficiently while holding onto tradition, then it seemed like pulling a wagon would be an ideal way to build crew unity and bring a lot of recognition to the ranch. Additionally, cowboys have a longing to be in the wild.

For those of you not familiar with wagon works, we would leave headquarters with a chuck wagon, a crew of 12 men and about 85 head of saddle horses. We would find a convenient spot between three or four pastures and camp out there while we were branding the calves. After working cattle in those pastures, we would move camp to the next location to brand more calves. In our case, with the size of the ranch, the process would take approximately four to five weeks to get around to all the pastures. Of course we stashed a vehicle at camp so the men could drive home to spend Sundays with their families and take a shower. Other than that, it was the Wild West.

I'll never forget the excitement of the crew when we pulled out the first time. I think we were so excited we made our first camp several hours before we had planned and had to sit around and wait for the sun to go down to start works the next day. Nightfall brought no relief, however. I don't think a single one of us slept. Why were we so excited? It was because we were in our element. We were back in the wild, out of the garden, where God purposely created us. Eve, however, was created in the garden and thus doesn't have the same longing. I'll never forget what my wife said the night before we left: "Are you ready for your glorified camping trip yet?"

It's the same reason I led 20 of my closest friends and family on a 15-mile, four-day packing trip in the Pecos Wilderness last summer. The ages of the participants ranged from 12 to 72, and each man was enthusiastic—excited to be away from the man-made, microwavable society we live in today. Regardless of their faith walk, each man had an indelible desire to be in God's creation, and in God's creation we were. I have never seen a more beautiful spot in my life. It's not just me, however. I opened this month's copy of *Western Horseman* last night, and practically the whole edition was dedicated to backcountry packing. I watched the movie Unbranded with my daughter a few evenings ago. Not only did the four men in that movie have a longing to go packing, but they took it to an extreme. They decided they would adopt mustangs, train them for four months and then ride from Mexico to Canada. Talk about a longing to be in the wild.

This wilderness that we were created in has incredible scriptural relevance as well. Several times when God needed to deal with man, He sent him to the wilderness. "So Moses brought Israel from the Red Sea; then they went out into the Wilderness of Shur. And they went three days in the wilderness and found no water" (Exodus 15:22 NIV). He also sent Jesus to the wilderness as a man (Matthew 4:1-11) to be tempted. In both occasions, God used the place where man was created to test them and strengthen their determination and faith in the Most High God. We don't serve a low-fat, precooked, microwavable God. We serve a mighty God who is not only familiar with our longing to be wild, but He is also intimate with it.

Day 3
"Valorous"

"And the Angel of the LORD appeared to him, and said to him, "The LORD is with you, you mighty man of valor"" (Judges 6:12 NKJV)

I was watching a video of a friend of mine, Quentin Marburger, for a TV show called Cowboy Authentic a few days ago. To paraphrase him, Quentin said that on the ranch where he worked the men strived to be men of valor, just like the above scripture describes. He went on to say that as cowboys they would fight for each other and have each other's backs. If you know Quentin, you know he is definitely not a fighting man, but he would stand up for himself if he was backed into a corner. In his comments, I believe he was talking about the respect that each cowboy has for one another. See, on the ranch there are certain instances where a cowboy needs his back covered. Take for instance picking up a particularly bad bull or loading an old trotty cow. When you get into a situation like that, it's comforting to know that there is a cowboy with you who is worth his salt. However, it's more comforting to know that cowboy is also a mighty man of valor.

Most books define valor as great courage in the face of danger, especially in battle. I like Merriam-Webster's definition of valor: strength of mind or spirit that enables a person to encounter danger with firmness. If God called Gideon a mighty man of valor in the book of Judges, and Quentin says that the men on a ranch in the rolling hills of West Texas strive to be men of valor, then I ask you the very simple question: who are we? More importantly, why are we striving to be like a man of the Old Testament who lived thousands of years ago? If you look to the Bible, the answers are very clear. We are quite simply the same man that our Father created in Adam, and it is written in our DNA to have the very same qualities and attributes that he and Gideon and Sampson and many others had as well. If you want an example of a man of great courage in the face of danger, use Sampson. The following verse comes after Sampson finds out that the Philistines have burned his wife to death. "When he came to Lehi, the Philistines came shouting against him. Then the Spirit of the LORD came mightily upon him; and the ropes that were on his arms became like flax that is burned with fire, and his bonds broke loose from his hands. He found a fresh jawbone of a donkey, reached out his hand and took it, and killed a thousand men with it" (Judges 15:14-15, NKJV). "Wait! Hold on," you say. "I didn't learn about that in Sunday school. Are your sure you are reading the same Bible that I have over there on the mantle?" Of course I am. Maybe you want to shrug it off to simply Old Testament barbarism. If that's so, then how do you explain, "And from the days of John the Baptist until now the kingdom of heaven suffers violence, and the violent take it by force"(Matthew 11:12 NKJV).

So, the Philistines have likely not murdered your wife, and the Lord has likely not asked you to defeat thousands with three hundred men as He instructed Gideon. However, make no mistake that you and I and every man was born with the DNA of Adam, and it contains the valor as shown by Sampson and Gideon. So, maybe you are asking yourself why the Lord would give you such valor, and why you would ever need it. I believe there will be a time that comes in every man's life where he will be forced to test his valor. If the Philistines don't come for your wife or family, maybe sickness will. How will you respond to cancer or disease that comes upon you or your family? What about being the parent to a child with a disability, or being asked to defend your country? There will come a time when you will need to test your valor. Will you pick up the jawbone, or will you perish?

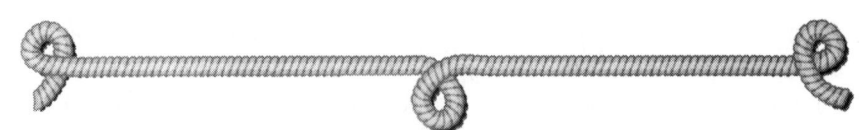

Day 4
"Bold"

"And when they had prayed, the place where they were assembled together was shaken; and they were all filled with the Holy Spirit, and they spoke the word of God with boldness" (Acts 4:31 NKJV).

Doing what most of us do for a living takes a certain amount of boldness. Let's face it, we are working with wild cattle from the backs of horses, which at one time were wild (and may still be), with wild men around us. I know what some of you are thinking about right now. "I'm glad I don't work for that outfit." Well, let me back up then. Many of us have been to the Beef Quality Assurance cattle handling workshops, and on a day-to-day basis we effectively and efficiently work our cattle slowly. But in big ranch country, even stockmanship guru Bud Williams has to pull his rope down on occasion, or employ someone who will. In the meadows up north you have to pull your rope down to doctor a calf, and certainly one must get a little bold on the wheat pastures of the plains. If we didn't have a certain amount of boldness and crave a little adventure, then we would be drying cars off at the wash in town. I've seen men in their mid-50s or later keep an old rogue horse in their string just to make sure they keep their edge.

Being bold is written into our nature. It's what God created us to be. Ask yourself for a second what language we would be speaking if our fathers and grandfathers had not been bold enough to invade Normandy on D-Day. Does your day go smoother when you are following a foreman or drive leader who is bold and decisive, or one who is timid and second-guesses himself? I bet we can all answer that question.

My occupation hasn't always been with a ranch. No, in one of my previous jobs, I worked as a professor at a university. About the boldest thing I did there was to decide between the Grande or Venti coffee in the morning. (I hope you know I am exaggerating for effect.) After several months of prayer and consulting with my wife, we decided to begin working on a ranch. My first job was as a camp cowboy at Matador Cattle Company in Matador, Texas. Since I had a Ph.D. in animal nutrition, I was in charge of the nutrition for the ranch as well. When I first started at Matador, I was as lost as a northbound duck in winter. I was out of my element, and it made me timid to boot. I was frustrated in my first few weeks, and my frustration came to a head one night when my wife, Cara, asked me, "Are you sure you can cowboy with these guys?" A few days later we were on the east side of the ranch and had found a set of tracks that led through a water gap that had been washed away. Like good cowboys, we decided we would check out what was going on at the neighbors for a little bit. In a short while, we crashed two pair of Matador "flying v" branded cows out of the brush that were wild as snakes. From the looks of it, their calves didn't fall too far from the tree. We threw them on a county road and decided that we would just load them off the gravel right-of-way. I was riding a three-year-old gelding that hadn't been ridden much, but when the boss pulled his rope out to tie-hard, I did the same. There were about five of us, and one cow kept shooting between us and getting away. We would systematically have to go and bring her back each time while we waited for the trailer to arrive. The second-to-last time she tried it, Tim said, "Next time, someone make her wear it." We were all standing in the middle of the gravel county road and she tried it another time. Fortuitously, she happened to pick my hole. I quartered my horse and let her have it without moving a step forward. Bay hadn't had much roped on him before that day, but as he went to his knees to absorb the shock, he sure learned a lesson in handling stock. We held her right where we caught her until someone pitched his rope on the heels. If there was any doubt I could cowboy with the crew, it was erased that day.

We don't have to ask permission to be bold, and we certainly don't have to apologize. Just like Peter and John, who shook the ground where they prayed, God gave us boldness and expects us to use it.

Day 5
"Reckless"

"However, I consider my life worth nothing to me; my only aim is to finish the race and complete the task the Lord Jesus has given me—the task of testifying to the good news of God's grace"
(Acts 20:24 NIV).

Have you ever……? Okay, let me back up. I know you have, so let me rephrase my question. Do you remember the time when you nearly blacked out and took off after that cow with reckless abandon through the mesquite or maybe the sage? She had been wrecking the drive all morning and would have loved to have scattered the entire herd. However, you lay in wait for her and tore after her through the brush and over the badger holes without caring about the consequences of your actions. She was going to go to the pens that day, and then you were going to load her up and take her to the butcher. Then you were going to bring the fresh hamburger home and cook a meal for your……. Excuse me. I got a little carried away; I too blacked out for a minute.

Since the beginning of the existence of cowboys, the word "cowboy" has almost been synonymous with reckless. The first cowboys essentially created it. I mean, who in their right mind would take a herd of squirrely longhorns hundreds of miles over uncharted territory only to fight Indians, rustlers, rogue horses and dysentery? It would definitely take a man who was a little reckless. The synonymy of the word "cowboy" with recklessness tickles me when used in world affairs today. Remember when several foreign leaders called George W. Bush a cowboy? They weren't referring to his boots.

What if I told you that God created us to have reckless abandon? You would probably respond with, "Well, your devotional has been entertaining for a few days, but this is where I lay it down." Stick with me for a bit while I give you an example. In fact the Apostle Paul, who penned the majority of the New Testament, was a man who was well versed in reckless abandon.

Remember, Paul who was first known as Saul, had been a persecutor of Christians. In fact, the purpose of his infamous walk to Damascus was so that he could arrest Christians who he thought were posing a threat to his religious tradition. Of course as you remember the story, the Lord came upon Paul in a mighty way and caused him to lose his eyesight. When Paul regained his eyesight, his life was never the same. "But the Lord said to Ananias, 'Go! This man is my chosen instrument to proclaim my name to the Gentiles and their kings and to the people of Israel. I will show him how much he must suffer for my name'" (Acts 9:15-16 NIV). And, suffer Paul did. Paul was arrested and imprisoned on multiple occasions. He was nearly stoned to death in Lystra and shipwrecked several times. He was beaten and scourged on multiple occasions, and finally was martyred for his devotion to Christianity. After Paul blacked out for a while, he opened his eyes and truly "blacked out" for Christ. He blindly preached and spread the Gospel of Christianity with reckless abandon. He obviously didn't care about the consequences of his actions. You can see that reading his own words. "For I am already being poured out like a drink offering, and the time for my departure is near. I have fought the good fight, I have finished the race, I have kept the faith. Now there is in store for me the crown of righteousness, which the Lord, the righteous Judge, will award to me on that day—and not only to me, but also to all who have longed for his appearing" (2 Timothy 4:6-8 NIV).

Yes, in the face of beatings, peril, imprisonment and impending death, the Apostle Paul was steadfast in his reckless abandon in spreading the gospel of Jesus Christ. In my book, Paul was the first cowboy.

Day 6
"Dedicated"

"Then you will call on me and come and pray to me, and I will listen to you. You will seek me and find me when you seek me with all your heart"
(Jeremiah 29:12-13 NIV).

    You have undoubtedly heard the phrase, "ride for the brand." Brands and the outfits they are associated with are symbols of pride and dedication. How many men have you seen out there that wear a brand on their buckle, bridle, saddle or leggings? Most working cowboys I know regard their trappings as some of their most prized items, so for them to adorn it with symbols of the outfits where they have worked means they have a great sense of pride or dedication. I recently had a man call me to ask if I knew about any position openings. This is a gentleman and a cowboy whom I respect very much. He had worked for some of the larger and more respected outfits in the Great Basin country. As he started to explain his situation, I knew I also respected him because of a great sense of personal dedication. The outfit he was working for had decided to close its doors. He had worked there for several years and had helped an absentee owner build a profitable enterprise out of a mismanaged outfit. The news was quite sudden as he and his family had laid down roots in the ranch and the community. He certainly had the right to pack up and leave them in the cold, or be angry with the situation, but he handled it much differently. When I asked him how long he would be staying at his current place of employment, he replied, "Well, we will be here until after calving. I am certainly not going to leave them until I finish that job." Think about that for a minute. He was being let go, and he had enough honor and dedication to not leave anything undone.

    Visiting with him reminded me of an open letter I saw once. This letter was pinned to the board in the break room at a feed yard. It reads like this:

If You Work for a Man

"If you work for a man, in Heaven's name work for him. If he pays you wages that supply your bread and butter, work for him, speak well of him, think well of him, and stand by him, and stand by the institution he represents. Do not work for him a part of his time, but all of his time. Give him undivided service, or none. If put to the pinch, an ounce of loyalty is worth a pound of cleverness. If you must vilify, condemn, and eternally disparage, then resign your position, and when you are outside, damn to your heart's content. But, so long as you are a part of an institution, do not condemn it. Not that you will injure the institution, but when you disparage the concern of which you are a part, you disparage yourself." -- Unknown

When I first read this, it made the hair on the back of my neck stand up in that same way that it does every time I hear the Star Spangled Banner sung at an event, or the same way it does every time I see our soldiers fighting for freedom. Having dedication takes humility and believing in a cause that is bigger than yourself. That takes building people up around you for the betterment of the cause.

We come by this sense of dedication honestly. Our Father was so dedicated to us, He sent His only son to die for us, so that we may have eternal life. "Be strong and courageous. Do not be afraid or terrified because of them, for the Lord your God goes with you; he will never leave you nor forsake you" (Deuteronomy 31:6 NIV).

If you are a Christian there is no need to wear symbols of Christianity. People will be able to see your brand by the way you talk and the way you live your life. Will you ride for the brand of the Lord?

Day 7
"Honorable"

"Pray for us. We are sure that we have a clear conscience and desire to live honorably in every way" (Hebrews 13:18 NIV).

I am sure many of you have seen both versions of the film, but my son, Grady, really likes the remake of Monte Walsh. We have watched it several times. We were watching one evening when a particular part that I had seen many times hit me pretty profoundly. The crew from the Slash Y were gathering some horses and driving them to a railhead. As they approached the loading pens the steam engine was boiling and ready to fire. The horses were ready to fire as well. Anyone who has ever cowboyed for a living knows the exact feeling that the crew from the Slash Y was feeling at that moment. "Easy, just a little further guys, hang in there with us." There is a critical point when you are trying to gather steers to ship off of wheat, or a set of spoiled cows to a branding pen, when it's either do or die. There are a few split seconds in there where it's either gonna happen or it's not. Well, the boys from that crew were right there, when the train engineer thought it would be funny to blow the horn. And, I'm sure that's also happened to you. Just in that moment when you are about to pen those steers off wheat, a truck driver slams a cut gate, or just when you are about to pen those spoiled cows a photographer swings around in front of them and they split to high hell. Well, if it has, then you know that feeling you get down in your stomach when your prize splits in about 47 different directions after a morning of hard work gathering and driving them to the pens. Well, in the movie the boys from the Slash Y decide to take matters into their own hands. They rope the stack on the steam engine and pull it off, thus rendering the giant train useless. When word gets back to the absentee accountant for the ranch, he approaches the manager about the cowboys paying for the damages. After much disagreement, he demands that the cowboys will pay for the damages. The manager stands his ground and says, "They are not gonna pay. Our men make $25 a week, and they buy their own gear. They aren't gonna pay." The accountant tries threatening the manager with his job, but he doesn't budge. Then the accountant says, "You would lose your job for these men?" The manager subsequently says, "I'd lose my life for them, and they'd do the same for me."

For the past three years, I have been in and out of hospitals and doctor visits. I been cut on, irradiated, discouraged and nearly broken. Yet, my crew has never wavered. For the last three years, we have weaned the biggest calves the ranch has ever had and had the highest calf crop percentage since I've worked for the ranch. We have also built a functioning feed mill from scratch, and increased our yields on both farms among countless other projects and achievements. And it's not just the men on the ranch either. The women have stepped up as well, keeping our kids while Cara and I have been away, and they have demonstrated countless other acts of love and dedication. I consider them just as much a part of the "crew" as the men. When I can work, they allow me to slide in seamlessly as if I hadn't missed a day, and when I am away I no longer worry about what's getting done, because I know they have pride in what they do. Yes, I'd gladly lose my life for them, and they'd do the same for me. It reminds me of the verse, "Then Simon Peter, having a sword, drew it and struck the high priest's servant, and cut off his right ear. The servant's name was Malchus" (John 18:10 NKJV). I am by no way comparing myself to our Savior, but I know the feeling that He felt when Peter drew his sword. We have dozens of men and women around us on the ranch and off the ranch with their spiritual swords drawn for us.

The love, dedication and respect shown by my crew is due to honor. They honor me because I honor them. From my assistant managers right down to the guy who cuts the grass. I have respect and honor for every one of them. Honor is also intertwined into our DNA. Our Savior displayed the best examples of honor in the way He lived his life and how He treated the people around Him.

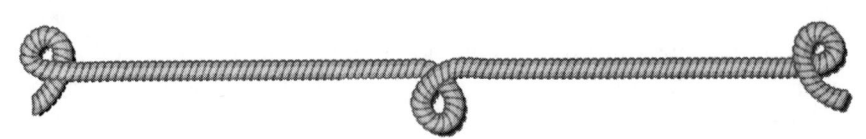

Day 8
"Longing to be a Cowboy"

"My soul yearns for you in the night; in the morning my spirit longs for you. When your judgments come upon the earth, the people of the world learn righteousness" (Isaiah 26:9 NIV).

Every red-blooded American boy asks the same question of themselves. Do I have what it takes? Can I be fierce? Really, think about it. I have a five-year-old son, and all he can think about is how he can be dangerous. We have bought him cowboy outfits and Native-American outfits and football outfits to name a few. Each one of them is equipped with the necessary guns, bows, helmets and pads. His day is consumed with daydreams of how he can shoot something, stab an arrow or knife in something, or run someone over in order to score a touchdown. Are we as men much different? I have a rifle or pistol for every occasion. Hunting and shooting sports is at an all-time high. Don't believe me, just take a trip to Cabela's or Gander Mountain. Does this make us weird or deranged? Not at all. Remember, we are made in the image of God; He created us. Each one of us that makes our living as working cowboys also have the same longing. We have a longing to be a cowboy. We must, because we all know that there are higher paying jobs out there with more downtime and freedom. Yet, we choose to wake up in the middle of the night in a blizzard to go assist a heifer that is having a calf. Or we choose to trot seven miles to the back of the pasture to gather it, rather than trailer. Why? Because we would rather do it that way. We would rather satisfy our longing than have a comfortable job in town. Don't get me wrong. The men in town also have a longing to be fierce. Many of them also have a longing to be cowboys, but they simply didn't follow that longing. Remember the movie City Slickers? That's a perfect example of men from the city who had a longing to do what we are blessed to do every day.

I spent my college years chasing what I thought was my longing. I was very focused, and without any breaks or time off I went 10 straight years from high school graduation to a Ph.D. I then went straight from a Ph.D. to an Assistant Professor position at a prestigious agricultural university. I was making a good living, everyone called me Dr. Wilson, and everything was right with my soul. Right? Wrong. While I loved to teach and interact with the students, everything went rapidly wrong. First of all, I was not cut out for the tenure process. The thought that you could work hard for a few years and then coast for the rest of your time really upset me. I wanted to be evaluated on a continual basis. Was I adding value to this place? If not, then I needed to hit the road. I also couldn't relate to the intellectual egos of some of my coworkers. I can say this with sincere honesty. I have had more intelligent conversations in my cowboy crew meetings than I ever did at a faculty meeting. However, the most piercing question that haunted me was simple. Did I have what it takes? The old adage of "professors teach because they can't do" haunted me. Was I like the rest of these guys, or could I really do? After a year of prayer, consultation with my wife and a lot communion with my Savior, I decided to take a leap of faith. I applied at a ranch to be a camp manager. Basically, I was to be a cowboy like the rest of the crew. At first, the manager who hired me thought I was crazy. After I took about a third of the pay to chase this longing, I thought I was crazy. However, I have never regretted my decision one day after leaving. Most of the people I worked with at the university were wonderful, gifted people and they were exactly where they needed and wanted to be. I had a longing to be outside in God's creation. I had a longing to feel the sun on my face and the wind at my back. I had a longing to be tested every day; a longing to prove that I could actually do what I had taught. I had a longing to be valorous, bold, reckless, dedicated and honorable. I had a longing to be a cowboy.

Day 9
"No Apology Needed"

"Have you been supposing [all this time] that we have been defending ourselves and apologizing to you? [It is] in the sight and the [very] presence of God [and as one] in Christ (the Messiah) that we have been speaking, dearly beloved, and all in order to build you up [spiritually]" (2 Corinthians 12:19 AMP).

If by chance you haven't quit me yet, I hope that I have convinced you that we are created in the image of God, we were created in the wilderness and naturally have the attributes of valor, boldness, recklessness, dedication and honor. And it is very much these qualities that give us a longing to be and do what we do. If that's so, then why should I need to go any further? If you and I both believe that, then why do we need 31 more days of this? The reason is that you don't truly believe it. I don't either, at least not all the time. The truth is that most of the time instead of behaving with valor, I show cowardice. Instead of displaying boldness and recklessness, I show meekness and control. Instead of being dedicated and honorable, I am uncommitted and shameful. Remember day 1? I said I would expose myself. Well here you go. It's time that we start getting real with each other.

The truth is that our culture has almost discredited the union of a good, Christian man and a cowboy. Really, think about it for a minute. Think about the popular cowboys you grew up idolizing. How often did the Duke offer a prayer before a meal? Even in Pale Rider, Clint Eastwood was a little rough around the edges as a preacher. You say you didn't idolize those guys. Fair enough. Rarely did I see any of the rodeo greats go to the podium to receive their prize and give praise to the Lord first. You say you didn't idolize those guys. Fair enough. You say that you were raised by a father or uncle or grandfather who was a God-fearing man and demanded that of you too. That's great, but extremely rare.

However, today we are starting to see a group of men unapologetically stand up and say that they are Christians and cowboys alike. These men are Jeff Gore, Steve Friskup and Ron Brunson, to name just a few. No, our culture has not welcomed it with open arms. Our culture has suggested that an apology was needed if you were anything other than what it considered a cowboy.

One time as we were headed back from a successful ranch rodeo at the Houston Livestock Show, something very profound happened in the pickup. About two hours from the house, one of our team members who was sitting in the back seat brought up a Bible study that he and his wife were hosting at their house. Have you ever seen a prairie fire? Well, his conversation starter was like a match thrown on the prairie on a windy day. For the next two hours our pickup opened up with some really deep and substantial conversation about Christianity. "Wait, hold on," you say. "I thought pickups driving to and from rodeos are supposed to be full of beer, pickled eggs, vulgarity, profanity, gas and the like, huh?" Not exactly. I had as deep and open of a conversation with those three guys about what God means to my life as I have ever had with anyone. I got into how that ties to my health, and I'm glad it was dark in there so the other guys couldn't see the tears streaming down my face.

Why is this so rare? Why do cowboys have to hide their Christianity? Why do many only come to the Lord on their death bed? It doesn't have to be this way. Listen, there is no apology needed. But, first we have to find what we have been missing. We have to find our bottom. We have to find our heart. I believe there are three things we have to learn to do. We have to learn to fight for our heart. We have to learn to live. And we have find our Eve.

I'll explain those important tasks during the next three days.

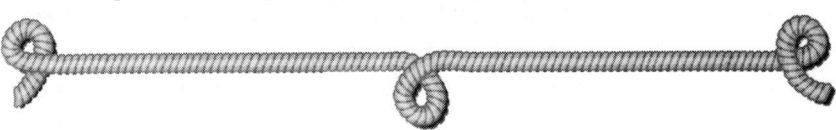

Day 10
"Fighting For Your Heart"

"Then Moses and the Israelites sang this song to the Lord: 'I will sing to the Lord, for he is highly exalted. Both horse and driver he has hurled into the sea. The Lord is my strength and my defense; he has become my salvation. He is my God, and I will praise him, my father's God, and I will exalt him. The Lord is a warrior; the Lord is his name'" (Exodus 15:1-3 NIV).

How did we go from being a society of learning to be champions and winners to becoming a society where everyone gets a trophy? I'm going to tell a story about one of my closest friends. The Fort Worth Stock Show and Rodeo invited one of our ranch kids to compete in the Mutton Busting during its Ranching Heritage Weekend one year. I asked my friend if his son wanted to represent the ranch. His son, who was about five at the time, was overjoyed, and that was all he could talk about for months leading up to the rodeo. He got all the necessary gear and was ready to perform under the big lights. Well, the night came and in front of about 5,000 people he made his way to the mutton chute. But all of a sudden he balked. I can't say that I blame him. Sometimes I think we as parents do it for ourselves instead of for the kids. His dad was frustrated and tried to lead him back to the chutes, but there was no way his son was getting on that night. They turned his sheep out and all the kids proceeded to the other end of the arena to get their trophies and take pictures. They gave my friend's son a trophy, just like all the rest of the kids who participated. However, after they got back to the seats, my friend took the trophy from his son. He was going to teach him a lesson. They brought the trophy home, and instead of putting it in the boy's room they put it on a high shelf in the living room to remind him that if he doesn't finish, then he doesn't get a trophy. I'm sure educated elites would like to criticize his parenting. I think he should receive an award for Dad of the Year!

Young boys grow up wanting to be powerful and dangerous, something to be reckoned with. However, we have decided as a society that that type of man is too dangerous. So we decide to cage him, to castrate him, so to speak. No, many people in our society don't want our boys to grow up as stallions; geldings would suit them much better. When my son was about two months old, I bought him his first pair of leggings. Of course he couldn't wear them, but he's now five and still wearing them. My father-in-law bought him a BB gun when he was three, and a close family friend got him a pocket knife a couple months ago. These are both gifts that will remain on the shelf for a while. Yet, my point is that our friends and family realize that we want to raise a man.

I have a friend who was raised on a famous ranch in the Panhandle of West Texas. He told me that he was nearly 30 years old before he was allowed to drag a calf during branding. If we want our sons and daughters to grow up with the same desires that we have, then why do we hobble them? Last year we had a kids' day on the ranch. We decided to take our time and let the kids do as much as they could one day during branding. One of my best friends and assistant manager, Zack Burson said, "I don't care if it takes all day, we are going to share with these kids the heritage we love so much."

Your heart is not just something that is given to you. No, you have to fight for it. The Lord is a warrior, and we are created in His image. We are designed to be men, and our boys are destined to be men. So encourage them.

Last year, one evening just before dark, I had the privilege of penning a yearling bull with my son. He had never ridden in the pasture without me ponying him. I let him loose, and we moved the bull a couple miles back to the heifers where he belonged. Not a week goes by that my son doesn't talk about that day. I can honestly say that it was the best day of my life.

To transition from who we are to who we want to be, we must learn to fight for our hearts. We must learn to be the men and cowboys that God created us to be.

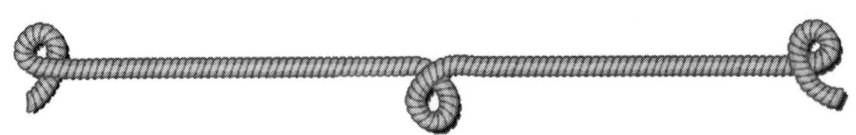

Day 11
"Learning to Live"

"For where your treasure is, there your heart will be also" (Matthew 6:21 NIV).

I'm sure many of you have either watched the movie or read the book All the Pretty Horses. It is one of my absolute favorites. John Grady Cole and Lacey Rawlins are two 16-year-old boys who quickly turn into men. They leave their home in Texas and ride to Mexico on an adventure bigger than their native state. They get a job on a ranch in Mexico and on their third day they are taken to a holding pen with 16 wild and visibly spooked young horses. John Grady looks the horses over and says, "You think me and you could break all them in four days?" Rawlins asks, "Why four days?" John Grady quickly replies, "Ya think we could do it?" Rawlins takes another look, a longer one this time, and says, "You'd be about a worn out sum buck, I'll tell you that." The two are cowboys alright, and they are raring for an adventure. They are learning to live. Living an adventure is at the core of every man's soul. It's at the core of every man's heart, and finding an adventure is the secret to unlocking a man's heart. It's what makes you come alive. The two tackle the job and ultimately win over the hearts and minds of the Hispanic cowboys and their families. Before the scene is done, they have quite a following cheering them on.

Why do many of us miss our adventure? Some cowboys grasp this concept very readily and all their stories begin with the preface, "You're not gonna believe this stuff." Learning to live requires something of us, and constantly living an adventure continually puts us to the test. Now every one of us is born with this desire. Take little boys for example. How many little boys have you seen with cap guns strapped to their hips? One year for his birthday, all my son really wanted was a badge. He would walk around saying, "I'm the sheriff of this town." So if we are born with it, then where does it go for most men? Many times it goes away because our false self requires an outcome before we engage. An adventure is just that: unknown. But, some decide that they don't want any part of it. Likely that is because they believe they will fail the test. They want to know the outcome before they engage. That reminds me of my favorite quote of all time.

It's not the critic that counts; not the man who points out how the strong man stumbles, or where the doer of deeds could have done them better. The credit belongs to the man in the arena, whose face is marred by dust and sweat and blood; who strives valiantly, who errs, who comes short again and again, because there is no effort without error and shortcoming; but who does actually strive to do the deeds; who knows great enthusiasms, and great devotions, who spends himself in a worthy cause; who at the best knows in the end the triumph of high achievement, and who at the worst, if he fails, at least he fails while daring greatly; so that his place shall never be with those cold and timid souls, who neither know victory nor defeat.
—Theodore Roosevelt

Teddy knew how to live. Just remember the story of his Rough Riders leading the charge up San Juan Hill? His bravery that day earned him a Medal of Honor and ultimately the presidency. His bravery and willingness to live didn't end that day, however. No, he spent the rest of his life living one adventure after another.

Don't get me wrong on this one. Some men will take this as permission to do the wrong things. Learning to live is not running off with that woman you saw at the rodeo last weekend. That is cowardice. A real adventure is learning how to forever love and support your wife and family. A real adventure is trusting God. In order to trust Him, you have to let go and let Him. You have to turn the reins over to Him. Those of you who have been to a point where you have no other choice but to give it all to Him, yes, you know what real adventure is. You know what truly makes you come alive.

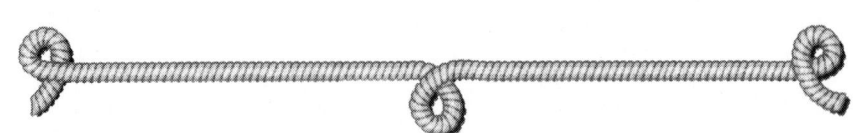

Day 12
"Finding Your Eve"

"The Lord God said, 'It is not good for the man to be alone. I will make a helper suitable for him.' So the man gave names to all the livestock, the birds in the sky and all the wild animals. But for Adam no suitable helper was found. So the Lord God caused the man to fall into a deep sleep; and while he was sleeping, he took one of the man's ribs and then closed up the place with flesh. Then the Lord God made a woman from the rib he had taken out of the man, and he brought her to the man. The man said, 'This is now bone of my bones and flesh of my flesh; she shall be called "woman," for she was taken out of man"'
(Genesis 2:18, 20-23 NIV).

How many western movies have you seen where the plot is centered on the romance of a man and woman, or the main character has a romance with a woman aside from the main plot? A lot, huh? In fact, it's hard to think of many that don't. It always tickles me when John Wayne grabs up the woman in his movies and kisses her forcefully. Just for fun, I try that with my wife Cara sometimes. For the record, it doesn't work as well for me. However, it's not just western movies or movies at all. Over history, wars have been waged and lives lost over the beauty of women. Just take Helen of Troy for example.

Why is this? What could drive a man so crazy that he would willingly lose life and property for a woman, and what would make the same scenario repeat over and over in history? It's actually very simple. God made Eve for Adam. God made woman for man. When boys come of age and realize this, it simply turns their lives upside down. We lived in Las Vegas, Nevada, when I was in junior high, and I had my eye on this girl at school. But I was really shy and hadn't talked to her much. When we lived there, I was zoned for a really large inner-city school, and I was a bit of an outcast. I wore Wranglers and collared shirts to class, and apparently that wasn't the hip thing to do. We were roping at a neighbor's arena and she happened to be visiting a friend that lived a couple houses away for the weekend. I hadn't been roping very well that day, but as she walked up everything changed. I instantaneously went from roping very few to roping like Clay O'Brien Cooper. Honestly, you could have backed me in the box at the Thomas and Mack and I would have won money. Why is that? It's because cowboys naturally want to be heroes, and in our minds only champions win the prize.

If men are so enamored with women, then why are there so many divorces and infidelity in marriages? Some men spend time, money, sweat and tears trying to woo their bride only to leave her 7 years later because he says, "She is just not the same woman I married." Or, he stops pursuing her, and someone from her work fills the void. The woman says, "He treats me like my husband did when we were dating." Both instances stem from the same basic problems. A woman wants to know she is beautiful, and a man wants to pursue his Eve. Once that is lost, you can almost call off all bets.

I dated a girl in high-school and college whose father was an incredibly brilliant man. He wrote a book once that was very profound to me. In the book, he told a story of his first wife who had died of cancer. During her battle, she had to have a double mastectomy. She was obviously distraught about the cancer and surgery, but deep down her biggest fear was that after the surgery she would not be beautiful any longer. When she came to in the recovery room, he was waiting on her and she started to cry. He said, "Why are you crying, are you in pain?" She said, "No, I am no longer beautiful and you will no longer want me." The man immediately took her bandages off, knelt down and kissed her chest and said, "You are even more beautiful and you ever were before." Cowboys, that's a man. He was committed to pursuing and fighting for his woman. Will you fight for your Eve?

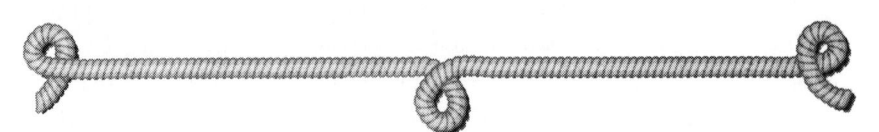

Unit 2
Why We Are

Day 13
"Where Did It All Go Wrong"

"Therefore, just as sin entered the world through one man, and death through sin, and in this way death came to all people, because all sinned—"
(Romans 5:12 NIV).

"Surely I was sinful at birth, sinful from the time my mother conceived me"
(Psalm 51:5 NIV).

"The Lord looks down from heaven on all mankind to see if there are any who understand, any who seek God. All have turned away, all have become corrupt; there is no one who does good, not even one" (Psalm 14:2-3 NIV).

For the first 12 days we have focused on what we are and the virtues bestowed upon us from our Creator. When we study who He is, it's not too far-fetched to understand why we are the cowboys that we are and how we act and interact with those around us. Because it was the virtues of valor, boldness, honor and the like bestowed upon us by Him, they were thus the good side of us. The white-hatted side of us, so to speak. The side we don't mind talking about and sharing with others. But the real truth is that we have scars. We have visible scars, and we have inner scars that cut so deep it seems as though they may never diminish. For the next several days, we are going to focus on those scars. Like I said on Day 1, I am going to expose myself, and if you are honest with yourself, you will be exposed too.

The three verses above deal with a concept that theologians love to disagree about called "original sin." Some theologians believe that every person, every child, is automatically born a sinner. By their line of thinking you come out of your mother's womb a sinner. It's interwoven in our DNA that we inherited from Adam and Eve. Other theologians believe that you don't come out of the womb a sinner, but once a person has the cognitive ability to reason, they will sin and fall short of the glory of God. Having raised children, it is amazing to me that no matter how hard you try to raise them right, they will learn to lie and try to manipulate you at an early age. I'm not here to argue the validity of either side, and I am certainly not a theologian. However, I know that there was only one person ever born to this life who was blameless and thus free from sin. That person was Jesus Christ the man.

Let's go back to Genesis 3. The serpent (Satan) catches Eve in the Garden of Eden and tempts her to eat from the only tree that God had instructed Adam not to eat from. Adam has surely relayed the message to Eve and she has heard about the consequences, but the serpent tricks her into eating from the tree. The end of verse 6 says, "She also gave some to her husband, who was with her, and he ate it" (Genesis 3:6 NIV). We could spend a whole study on this chapter, but I think it is very significant that God created Eve after He told Adam about the fruit, and Eve was the one tempted by the serpent. It was Adam's job to communicate to his wife that she was not to eat from the tree. Does your wife ever express to you that you have poor communication skills? Likewise, the serpent tempted Eve and not Adam. I have no basis for this, but somewhere deep inside I believe that Adam may not have been tempted, but there is no way he could say no to the love of his life. Don't get me wrong. I am not disparaging Eve, as I am easily tempted myself. But Satan, being very crafty, knew that Adam would not say no to his wife. Anyone, have a problem with this today? Thus, here we are, sinners. The sin of one man and one woman changed the course of humanity. That sin is the reason we have broken homes and broken families. The reason we have lost loved ones and lost lives.

The only way to escape this perpetual sin is to come to know Jesus Christ as your Savior and repent from your ways. Over the next several days, we will work through this sin and how He has instructed us to overcome it.

Day 14
"The Spread of Sin In Man"

"We know that the whole creation has been groaning as in the pains of childbirth right up to the present time" (Romans 8:22 NIV).

Little did Adam and Eve know that the sin they brought into the Garden of Eden would quickly spread. They would be the literal creators of sin, known as generational sin. We pick up the story in Genesis Chapter 4, and we find out that Adam and Eve first have a son named Cain, then later have a son named Abel. We don't know how quickly after, but I believe we can easily conclude that they were close in age. The text goes on to say that Cain was a farmer and Abel was a shepherd. After Adam and Eve had sinned, God evicted them from the garden and told Adam that he would forever have to work for his food. "To Adam he said, 'Because you listened to your wife and ate fruit from the tree about which I commanded you, "You must not eat from it," Cursed is the ground because of you; through painful toil you will eat food from it all the days of your life. It will produce thorns and thistles for you, and you will eat the plants of the field. By the sweat of your brow you will eat your food until you return to the ground, since from it you were taken; for dust you are and to dust you will return' " (Genesis 3:17-19 NIV). Thus was the inception of modern agriculture. It won't do you any good, but as you build fence in the 100 degree heat, bale hay at midnight to catch the right moisture, calve heifers in the driving snowstorm and water-gap to your waist after a flood, you can blame Adam to your heart's content.

When it came for the brothers to give an offering of the fruits of their labor to God, in faith Abel offered the very best of his flocks to be pleasing to God. Cain obviously did not do the same with his offering. The chapter doesn't exactly say what Cain offered, but God was obviously displeased with him. Let's pick up the text there. "Then the Lord said to Cain, 'Why are you angry? Why is your face downcast? If you do what is right, will you not be accepted? But if you do not do what is right, sin is crouching at your door; it desires to have you, but you must rule over it.' Now Cain said to his brother Abel, 'Let's go out to the field.' While they were in the field, Cain attacked his brother Abel and killed him. Then the Lord said to Cain, 'Where is your brother Abel?' 'I don't know,' he replied. 'Am I my brother's keeper' " (Genesis 4:6-9 NIV)?

Whoa. When I read this, there is so very much wrong with it. First, how did we as mankind go from the first sin of eating an apple to the next sin of murder? Talk about escalation of sin! Secondly, nearly all that is wrong with humanity can be summed up by Cain's statement, "I don't know. Am I my brother's keeper?" Reading through that, I was expecting a big ol' backhand from God. At least that's what my daddy would have done. Instead, God stripped Cain of his ability to work the land and made him a wanderer. The escalation of sin wouldn't end there, however. It followed him and went from bad to worse. Through his lineage, sin spreads and escalates into the stories of the Great Flood and the Tower of Babel.

When we think about it this way, it's easy to view sin on a large scale and see how it has spread from generation to generation throughout humanity. However, it has a little more sting when we consider its role in our own lives. Go back to the text above. "But if you do not do what is right, sin is crouching at your door; it desires to have you, but you must rule over it" (Genesis 4:7). How easy is it to let a little sin in your life snowball into a bigger sin? We emphasize this on the ranch all the time with the men and women who work there. Obviously, when working on a ranch some things are provided to you. It may be a barn, feed, equipment and such for your personal horses. However, there is always a sinful opportunity to take advantage of those things. Let's say a man borrowed a bucket of feed from the ranch to feed some personal cows. That sin is not too big, but over the years it may turn into feeding herds of personal cows. A tank of company gas may turn into charging personal trips and vacations to the ranch. We must guard our hearts and flesh from all sin because the smallest, most insignificant sin can quickly escalate into the sin of Cain. Sin certainly is crouching to devour us, and we must rule over it.

Day 15
"The Great Cover-Up"

"Whoever conceals their sins does not prosper, but the one who confesses and renounces them finds mercy" (Proverbs 28:13 NIV).

"If I have covered my transgressions as Adam, by hiding my iniquity in my bosom" (Job 31:33 NKJV).

From the beginning of time, we have desired to cover up our sin. Let's pick it up again with Adam and Eve. "Then the eyes of both of them were opened, and they knew that they were naked; and they sewed fig leaves together and made themselves coverings. And they heard the sound of the LORD God walking in the garden in the cool of the day, and Adam and his wife hid themselves from the presence of the LORD God among the trees of the garden. Then the LORD God called to Adam and said to him, 'Where are you?' So he said, 'I heard Your voice in the garden, and I was afraid because I was naked; and I hid myself.' And He said, 'Who told you that you were naked? Have you eaten from the tree of which I commanded you that you should not eat' " (Genesis 3:7-11 NKJV)? The first couple had not been sinning very long, but they developed a conscience very quickly. They also developed shame and embarrassment as well. Why do we try to cover our sin? It is always one of two reasons. Like Adam and Eve, we are either embarrassed or ashamed by it, or we cover our sin to avoid punishment and consequences. We all have done it. I know sometimes I need a D-9 Cat to push enough fig leaves over some of my sins. How about other ways we try to cover our sin, however? What about the fig leaves of alcohol, busyness, food, entertainment, self-depreciation, and a host of other problems and addictions? If you go back to the scripture, I find something very comforting and somehow ironic. Although God loathes sin and certainly punishes mankind for it, He also had immediate compassion for the first humans. "The Lord God made garments of skin for Adam and his wife and clothed them" (Genesis 3:21 NIV).

Even though they tried to hide their sin from God, He was compassionate enough to help them cover the inequity of their sin. Just as God made the first covering for Adam and Eve, he also made the sacrifice of Jesus Christ on the cross for as a covering for our sin. So why do we cover up at all? It's for the obvious reasons above. However, we serve a forgiving God who knows that we are flawed and desires for us to come to him for forgiveness.

I had been working for Matador Cattle Company for only a few months, when I slept in one Sunday morning. We had just finished weaning or were nearing the end of it, and had been working very long days, six days a week. However, the horses still needed to be fed at headquarters, and it was my Sunday to do it. I was embarrassed for sleeping in and thought I would try to slip in unnoticed. As I pulled across the cattle guard, my boss, Bob Kilmer, met me on the road as he was driving to church. Bob casually asked what was going on and I quickly started hurling fig leaves. I explained to him that I had been out earlier, much earlier, and I was simply coming back to check on things again. Bob just smiled and drove on. As I continued on the road to the saddle house I realized that we had gotten a couple tenths of rain early that morning, and I didn't have enough fig leaves to cover my tracks to the barn. I was immediately devastated. I respected Bob so much, and I couldn't believe that I lied to him for absolutely no reason at all. I was beside myself and had to make it right. I caught Bob the first chance I got that afternoon and came clean to him. I told him that if he needed to let me go, I was ready to accept that consequence and that I would never lie to him again. He was so gracious that I had come to him and swallowed my pride, and he explained to me that Jesus desires that we confess our sins. I gained a whole new level of respect for Bob that afternoon, and I think even though I was in the wrong, he gained a whole new level of respect for me as well. I will never forget the lesson I learned that morning. Don't let your fig leaves pile so high they blind you from seeing and doing the right things.

Day 16
"Our Inadequacies"

"One day, after Moses had grown up, he went out to where his own people were and watched them at their hard labor. He saw an Egyptian beating a Hebrew, one of his own people. Looking this way and that and seeing no one, he killed the Egyptian and hid him in the sand. The next day he went out and saw two Hebrews fighting. He asked the one in the wrong, 'Why are you hitting your fellow Hebrew?' The man said, 'Who made you ruler and judge over us? Are you thinking of killing me as you killed the Egyptian?' Then Moses was afraid and thought, 'What I did must have become known'" (Exodus 2:11-14 NKJV).

Remember Day 1 when I asked you how you had the audacity to let your friends perish? I mean, you see them nearly every day. You call them your best friends. Surely you have had ample opportunities over the years to share your Christian experience with them. You have had these wonderful experiences of Christ in your own life and have witnessed miracles large and small, but you are going to let your buddy miss his ticket to eternal life because you don't have the gumption to witness. Do you want to know the truth? I was talking about myself. Yes, I have done this too many times to count. Why? Is it because I am not genuine and don't truly love my friends? Am I faking it? Not at all. Most of the time it's because I don't feel adequate. Who am I to be telling someone else how they should live their life? If only they could see what I have done over the course of my life. If they could see my scars of sin, then I would be exposed. Exposed as a farce, exposed as a liar and exposed as a sinner. The truth is that's no excuse because as we have learned in the last three days that we are all sinners. But God wants to equip and use each and every one of us. To illustrate this point, let's go back to the Old Testament again and study how Moses was called into action to save his own people.

From the scripture above, we find out that Moses is also far from being blameless. When exposed by the Hebrew man and condemned to death by

Pharaoh, Moses chose to flee and made a whole new life in a new land. The problem is that Moses could run from his former life, but he could not run from the calling that God had placed on his life. So, God funneled Moses to the wilderness so he could work on him a little. Imagine that. Let's pick up the text there. "There the angel of the Lord appeared to him in flames of fire from within a bush. Moses saw that though the bush was on fire it did not burn up" (Exodus 3:2 NIV). God came to Moses with a very clear sign and told him that his people were being persecuted. God was sending him to bring the Israelites out of Egypt. It doesn't say it in the text, but I am almost certain that Moses looked over both shoulders and pointed at himself and said, "Who, me?" The scripture continues, "But Moses said to God, 'Who am I that I should go to Pharaoh and bring the Israelites out of Egypt?' And God said, 'I will be with you. And this will be the sign to you that it is I who have sent you: When you have brought the people out of Egypt, you will worship God on this mountain' " (Exodus 11-12 NIV).

The rest of the story is, quite literally, history. But how do we apply it to our lives? We must realize that we all have inadequacies, we all fall short and we are all sinners. Yet, that doesn't give us the excuse not to follow the calling that each of us will be given. "Wait a minute!" you say. "I'm not cut out to be Billy Graham." I'm not asking you to. Is God? Not everyone is a great evangelical leader. But mark my word, everyone has a purpose, a Christian purpose in this life. Surely, those guys have led millions to Christ, but what about the person that led Billy Graham to Christ? Graham may have been the only one that person witnessed to, but that was their purpose, and their reward in heaven will be great nevertheless. Be a witness to those you love and to those you call friends. Don't let your pride and your inadequacies get in the way of their gift to spend eternal life with their Savior as well.

Day 17
"The Vices of Men"

"The acts of the flesh are obvious: sexual immorality, impurity and debauchery; idolatry and witchcraft; hatred, discord, jealousy, fits of rage, selfish ambition, dissensions, factions and envy; drunkenness, orgies, and the like. I warn you, as I did before, that those who live like this will not inherit the kingdom of God" (Galatians 5:19-21 NIV).

"For you have spent enough time in the past doing what pagans choose to do— living in debauchery, lust, drunkenness, orgies, carousing and detestable idolatry. They are surprised that you do not join them in their reckless, wild living, and they heap abuse on you. But they will have to give account to him who is ready to judge the living and the dead" (1 Peter 4:3-5 NIV).

I think a lot of people, and maybe cowboys in particular, pass over the scriptures above like they may the following scripture: "Abraham begot Isaac, Isaac begot Jacob, and Jacob begot Judah and his brothers. Judah begot Perez and Zerah by Tamar, Perez begot Hezron, and Hezron begot Ram" (Matthew 1:2-3 NKJV). You do have to admit that it softens the corrupt tone when you add words like puppies and cool mountain mornings to drunkenness and debauchery. Just ask Waylon and Willie when they sing Ed Bruce's old song. "A cowboy loves smoky ol' pool rooms and cool mountain mornings. Little warm puppies and children and girls of the night." Ah, what a nice guy you might think. Who doesn't like someone who likes puppies and children? Never mind the fact that he smells of smoke and spilt beer and was with a hooker last night. Now, don't start hurling rocks at me, because by no means am I hurling stone pieces of the Ten Commandments at you. I just wonder why our culture is given a pass on this stuff, or why so many guys think that if they don't participate, then they can't be let into the "cowboy club."

Don't believe me that some type of standard exists? How many westerns have you ever seen in your life where someone doesn't walk into the swinging doors of a barroom? How many modern rodeo events can you name that aren't endorsed by beer or liquor companies? Listen, I will be the first to tell you that I will enjoy a beer at the end of a hot day. For some, that's as far as it goes. But how many lives, families and homes have been wrecked by those of us who cannot enjoy just a beer or two at the end of the day? Instead, they ruin their lives and hurt those around them tormented by alcohol dependence.

How about your rodeo team member who introduced you to his new wife last week? She is number three or four, but you can't remember. When you ask him where he met her, he replies in his canned comment, "At the bar. Where else am I going to find them?" The truth is that's the culture we were raised in. Marshall Dillon didn't want to marry Miss Kitty because that meant too much commitment. Monte Walsh wanted to marry the hooker at the end of the movie before she passed. The Earp brothers of Tombstone did marry hookers. Ben and Howdy of The Rounders picked up the floozies off the side of the road instead of courting the rancher's daughters. Again, I'm not pointing a finger. Cara and I went dancing and partying at many a bar before and after we were married.

What I am asking is can we be cowboys and men? And not just men, but Godly men. "Sure," you say. Well, then why are so many of us wrapped up in pornography, lust and adultery? Why do we keep seeing ourselves and our friends lose their children to our own selfish desires? The reason is because it takes real men to make a commitment. With pornography and lust, men are just enjoying a woman at her expense. The man has nothing invested. We need more men who are invested and committed. Men who are committed to their wives and their children, committed to providing them with a life that is not corrupted by the vices of men. This world needs more men of valor, men who are bold, reckless, dedicated and honorable. Men who are humble enough to admit mistakes, ask for forgiveness and honor commitments. This world needs more real men; Godly men; Godly cowboys.

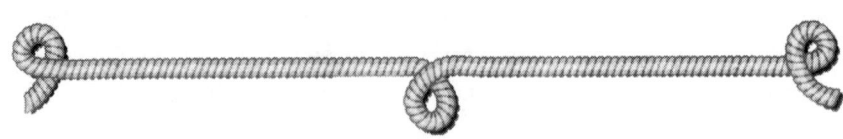

Day 18
"The Question that Haunts Us All"

"These things I have spoken to you, that in Me you may have peace. In the world you will have tribulation; but be of good cheer, I have overcome the world"
(John 16:33 NKJV).

Every single man deals with the following question: do I have what it takes? Do I have what it takes to be a cowboy? Do I have what it takes to be a man? This question doesn't just arrive unannounced one day when we decide to grow up. We as boys and young men are asking this question every day. How we answer that question, how we overcome adversity, and the confirmation we get from those who are closest to us, those things frame the rest of our lives.

Let's start with how we answer the question. It is largely written into our DNA and is influenced by the environment in which we live. I love asking people how their children, especially their boys, act when presented with this quandary. Most of the time, parents say that their oldest child is a little cautious when presented with challenges, and he is usually methodical and reasons his way through. The youngest are often entirely another ball of wax. They typically take challenges head on, not using their head to reason but using it to break the impending fall. Let's take my son, Grady, for example. He is our oldest. One year for his birthday his aunt and uncle got him a red bike. The bike was a little big, and when we set him on the seat, he was a long way from reaching the pedals. At first, he almost loathed the bike for that reason. On several occasions we encouraged him to ride it while we pushed, but his disapproving response was always, "That's a big boy's bike, Daddy." About a year passed, and his legs grew, and we caught him in there trying to pedal his bike. This time we backed off and let him take it at his own pace. In no time not only was he riding, but he soon came to us with a wrench and demanded that we take the training wheels off.

How we learn to overcome is pivotal in how successful we will be in life. I've always loved the saying, "It's doesn't matter how many times you fall, but what's important is how many times you get back up." I remember a story that a friend of mine recently told me. He was a young man and was starting a colt with his dad. The colt bucked him off and broke his arm. His dad's response was, "Get back on him so we don't spoil him, and then we can go get your arm fixed." Are you in shock? That was incredibly insensitive, right? Maybe, but he has grown into one of the most successful and persistent men I have ever known. He knows how to get back up.

The confirmation we get from those who are closest to us almost always comes from our dad or whomever standing in that gap for us, and there are always a pivotal moments when the question, "Do I have what it takes?" is answered for dad and ourselves. I was about 13 years old and Dad and I had been catching the occasional wild cow or bull for the local farmers. One afternoon one of the area nesters asked us to remove a neighbor's steer that had gotten in with his heifers. Instead of saddling his horse, Dad told me to hook up the pickup, saddle a horse and help the man myself. "Do I have what it takes without my dad?" I asked myself. I had never done the entire job without him. I didn't even have a driver's license. I drove to the man's place, caught the yearling steer, loaded it into the trailer and was out of there in approximately 20 minutes. Although it was a fairly simple task, it was the first all by myself. Dad sent me because he knew I could do it, and thus I knew I could do it. That was a pivotal moment for me as a young man answering that burning question.

Often your worldly father's confidence and confirmation is all it takes to build you up and help you answer the question. But, what happens when that confirmation breaks down? That's when you start developing your scars.

Day 19
"Our Father and Our Biggest Scar"

"Listen, my sons, to a father's instruction; pay attention and gain understanding. I give you sound learning, so do not forsake my teaching. For I too was a son to my father, still tender, and cherished by my mother. Then he taught me, and he said to me, 'Take hold of my words with all your heart; keep my commands, and you will live' " (Proverbs 4:1-4 NIV).

It is all too easy and unfortunately common that we take for granted the wisdom, love and understanding of our father. And why is it that when we are very young our father is our superhero, but we take him for granted when we are in our teens and early 20s? It often seems that we have to turn 30 before he becomes our superhero again. My father made a profound influence on me from a very young age. First of all, I have never met a harder working individual in my life. This is a virtue that I am very glad that he instilled in me. My father also taught me how to be compassionate to other people. I could go on and on about the bits of wisdom I learned from my father, but perhaps more important than wisdom, my father showed me how much he loved me. There is one occasion that I will never forget. I was about 11 or 12 and my dad and I were penning the roping steers down the alley next to the arena. It was about dark, and dad looked over at me and said, "Son, do you know who my favorite cowboy is?" I could only imagine who that could be. There were thousands of good choices. He quickly said, "You are." I could win every event imaginable and never feel as proud as I did that night. I never pass the opportunity to tell my son the very same thing.

The most profound part about my dad doing all this for me is that he didn't have to. He chose to, as he was actually my step-father. A lot of people are not as fortunate. Some men are not fortunate enough to have a father figure. I have a close friend who lost his father. We never talk about it, but I know it cuts him to the core. Some fathers are gone due to the breakdown of the family, which happens way too often. Some fathers are there, but lost to alcohol, drugs or their occupation. Some fathers are there, but they pass down the same demeaning insults and physical abuse they endured from their own father. No matter how good and honorable your father is, most likely your biggest scar will come from him.

Let me tell you about mine. I was 18 years old, and I was working with my father fulltime between high school graduation and my first year of college by helping train and show his clients' roping horses. I had been roping off a string of good horses at the shows all summer and had earned a fair amount of points on them. But, there was one horse that I really clicked with. Earlier when he was a stallion, he had gotten in a wreck and broke some of dad's ribs. After we castrated him, he made a good rope horse. But there was just something about him and me that really clicked in the show pen. At one of the biggest summer shows of the year I won high-point cattle horse on him, besting all the professional trainers. With that big win under my belt, I was ready for the World Championships later that summer. When the big show came around, however, I learned that a PRCA roper had been hired to show my best mount. I was beyond devastated. The question that haunted me was quickly answered. No, I was not good enough. I didn't have what it takes. I don't know if it was fate, but nevertheless it consoled my pride when the big-shot roper didn't catch a steer on him all day. It didn't heal my wound, however. It was a wound that developed into a scar and stayed with me for a long time. For several years, I pretty much quit competitive team roping all together. I got immersed college, and in the past five years I have finally begun roping again competitively.

Truth be told, I know that my dad was pressured by his clients to use a different roper that day. But it didn't hurt any less. I have completely forgiven him. Some men aren't as fortunate though. Some wounds left by their father don't heal for a long time. No matter how hard our earthly father tries, he is still human. Our dads can do a lot of things for us, but they just can't measure up to our true father without blemish, and that's our Father in Heaven.

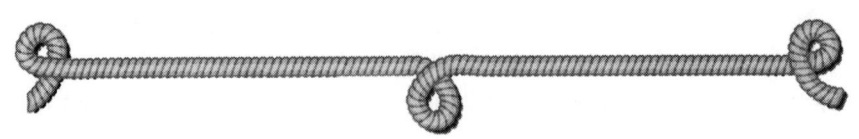

Day 20
"You Are A Lost Sheep"

"Suppose one of you has a hundred sheep and loses one of them. Doesn't he leave the ninety-nine in the open country and go after the lost sheep until he finds it? And when he finds it, he joyfully puts it on his shoulders and goes home. Then he calls his friends and neighbors together and says, 'Rejoice with me; I have found my lost sheep.' I tell you that in the same way there will be more rejoicing in heaven over one sinner who repents than over ninety-nine righteous persons who do not need to repent"
(Luke 15:4-7 NIV).

My grandmother was probably the toughest rancher's wife to ever live. When we were young, my grandfather was up in years and sick from heart failure. He had worked on several big outfits in Arizona, eastern New Mexico and the rolling plains and Panhandle of Texas. She had been through it all, right there with him cooking in bunkhouses, raising kids on meager pay and doing her fair share of the work. She was an amazing cook. I have never seen spreads like she put out on a routine basis. The beef was from a fatted calf, the milk and butter from the old ornery Hereford cow, and all the greens and vegetables were from her elaborate garden. You had also never seen so many pies and cakes. Every day was a like getting a meal during branding or fall shipping. Because of Granddad's age and poor health, my grandmother also handled a lot of the feeding and tending to the cows. Working in the bunkhouses on big outfits had instilled an uncanny level of toughness in her, and she fully understood cowboy dining room etiquette. If you didn't, she would train you to it quickly. I never realized I had such a disdain for sheep, but grandma's coined phrase always started, "You better clean your plate and set it next to the sink. You don't want to be a sheep herder." Well, I guess I didn't. At 5 years old, bright eyed with cowboy hat in tow and pistols strapped to my side, the last thing I wanted to be was a sheep herder.

I ran across the parable of the lost sheep while sitting in church the other day. Let's put it in the context of a heifer's calf, so we don't lose sight of the message. I know each one of you have been there. You know that heifer had a calf, you saw it and tagged it yesterday. Yet today you can't find it and she doesn't seem to care. Just like the parable, you spend the better part of the day, or maybe the rest of the night in a snow storm, trying to get them paired back up. Once you get them paired back up, you wipe the sweat off your brow, tally that accomplishment in your book, and feel like it's been a day well served. Meanwhile, you've got five more heifers calving, and one is down and needs assistance.

Are you that lost calf or sheep? Have you truly ever gotten over the scars of your youth? Don't underestimate the power of an old wound. Maybe you have never answered the question that haunts you. Or, you have answered it with, "No, I know I don't have what it takes." So, you have spent days, months or years as a lost sheep. You have turned to an addiction or addictions. You have engrossed yourself in your work or occupation. I know very strong men who have drifted off into a severe case of depression. That is nothing to scoff at. Maybe you have tried to get help.

If you are that lost sheep, I can tell you that our Lord Jesus Christ is searching for you right now. He is calling to you to come back to the herd. And, when He finds you, He will put you on His shoulders so high and will rejoice in the heavens. The only problem is, how do you help Him? Maybe you are seeking, too, but you can't find your way. You have been lost for years and are ready to find home. Most cowboys, even God-fearing men, are short on encouraging words because of their own insecurities. Some of us turn to church, and sometimes that plays right into the plan of the enemy.

Day 21
"Church"

"For it is by grace you have been saved, through faith—and this is not from yourselves, it is the gift of God— not by works, so that no one can boast"
(Ephesians 2:8-9 NIV).

So lost sheep, you went to church. What did you find there? Be honest with yourself. What did the women of the church look like? Did they look tired? Yeah, tired. Don't quit me yet. Just think about it. How often do many women of the church actually get fed on a weekly basis by the message? Not often. No, they are organizing activities, bringing lunch, trying to quiet kids, working in the nursery, singing with the praise and worship team, and the list goes on and on. A young mother with kids has already spent several hours getting herself and her kids ready even before she gets to the church. After all this work, is she being fed once she gets there? Not likely.

What about the men? What is a good church-going man supposed to look like? He is supposed to be dressed nicely, quiet and go through the motions. Yep, the modern church going man is supposed to be Mr. Rogers. How many of you men out there dreamed one day to be Mr. Rogers. The men of the church are subdued and obedient. Does God want it this way? No. So, how did we get this way?

Ever since the book of Acts, we sinning humans simply couldn't leave well enough alone. We have taken Christianity and turned it into a religion. "Back up," you say. "Christianity is the greatest religion of the world." I would say that Christianity is undoubtedly the greatest thing in the world, but in its truest form it is as far away from a religion as you can get. Let me share a story with you. Once I was in graduate school and was having a particularly hard time getting a certain lab assay to work. It had several meticulous steps, and I kept forgetting one or another. Each time it wouldn't go correctly, I would have to start over. So, I typed myself out a step-by-step procedure and put a box next to each step that I would have to check to make sure I had finished it. The last step said, "Pray to God that this works." One of my fellow classmates saw that, and she said, "I wish I could pray for you too but I am ...." I didn't write down the denomination because I don't want to disparage it, but it is a large, Christian-based one. I thought to myself, "My Jesus doesn't care what denomination you belong to, so how can your Jesus be so concerned with what denomination I belong to?" Basically folks, we have screwed it up. When Jesus said, "It is finished," He meant it. But no, we couldn't leave well enough alone. We put aside Moses' Law and made up a whole new set of our own laws.

So, have you ever walked into a church before and felt uncomfortable? Maybe you weren't dressed correctly, or maybe you didn't know when to kneel or what to say at the appropriate time. Maybe you sat in someone's pew or you just weren't righteous enough. Folks, that's not Jesus. We are broken and we are sinners and unfortunately we can't seem to keep our tendency to mess things up out of church. What has today's church done? It's driven many people away. I visited a beautiful gothic cathedral in Regensburg, Germany, that happened to be the church that Pope Benedict used to preside over. Unfortunately, there were more people in there taking pictures than there were people attending service, by a ratio of 5-to-1. It was a big, old, dead building. I also drove by a cowboy church outside of Wichita Falls once on a Sunday morning that had so many cars parked outside they flowed out of the parking lot and on the sides of the highway for several hundred yards. Why? Because cowboys have figured out a way to take legalism out of church. But, it's not just cowboys. I see it more and more all the time. How many non-denominational or Bible churches do you see around now? I see a lot.

I hope you have read down this far because here come the disclaimers. In no way am I disparaging your church, or church in general. The Church (that's all of us) is God's vehicle by which He spreads the Gospel to the world, and churches do an amazing amount of incredible work. But, don't allow your religion to drive a wedge between you and Christianity. I love my church, and I love to attend. But, if church is the only place that I am looking to engage Christ, then I am not going to get very far. Try taking the legalism and righteousness out of your religion and see how much closer you get to true Christianity. But, first we have to get over ourselves.

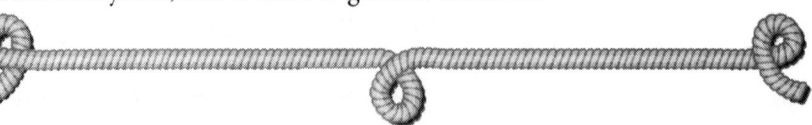

Day 22
"Let's Get Over Ourselves"

"As it is written: 'There is no one righteous, not even one; there is no one who understands; there is no one who seeks God. All have turned away, they have together become worthless; there is no one who does good, not even one. Their throats are open graves; their tongues practice deceit. The poison of vipers is on their lips. Their mouths are full of cursing and bitterness. Their feet are swift to shed blood; ruin and misery mark their ways, and the way of peace they do not know. There is no fear of God before their eyes.'...This righteousness is given through faith in Jesus Christ to all who believe. There is no difference between Jew and Gentile, for all have sinned and fall short of the glory of God, and all are justified freely by his grace through the redemption that came by Christ Jesus. God presented Christ as a sacrifice of atonement, through the shedding of his blood— to be received by faith. He did this to demonstrate his righteousness, because in his forbearance he had left the sins committed beforehand unpunished— he did it to demonstrate his righteousness at the present time, so as to be just and the one who justifies those who have faith in Jesus" (Romans 3:10-18, 22-26 NIV).

So it happens to everyone. If it hasn't happened to you yet, it will. One day you will find yourself at rock bottom, with no other "right" choice but to reach for Him, for Jesus Christ. I just went back and actually added the word "right" to that last sentence because I believe and know that people actually don't answer correctly when called in this life. Sometimes people are given the opportunity to seek Him in their time of need, but instead choose the ways of the evil one. But, mark His words, "For we all must appear before the judgment seat of Christ, so that each of us may receive what is due us for the things done while in the body, whether good or bad" (2 Corinthians 5:10 NIV). Mine came about 15 years ago. I was already a Christian, and I'm not saying that I have been perfect since, but back then I decided I needed to get over myself. "What does that mean," you say? It means that I was so selfish, so self-absorbent, so self-reliant, so caught up in my own righteousness that I couldn't see that I was a train wreck. Did I go to church? Sure, when it was convenient. Did I study the Bible? No. Did I seek Him? No, not until I realized that He was my only choice. I didn't consider myself wretched, and still don't, but I was definitely headed down the wrong path. See, I thought that I could do everything myself. I thought that I could right and wrong myself into a good life and to heaven. All it took was one adverse event in my life to realize that I had no control of my current life and much less my destiny. My only hope would be to put my faith in Him and lean on His understanding, not my own.

So what I am trying to say here folks is let's all just get over ourselves. Without Christ there is none righteous, no one who understands, no one who does good or can be good enough to have eternal life. And the funny thing is that what I thought was rock bottom at the time was nothing compared to what I have been through since. However, since I have found the One who sustains me and guides me, life's ups and downs are much easier to handle. It's easier to understand that life's valleys are simply attacks, and life's mountains are blessings. In both instances, we should go to the Lord for assistance or to give Him praise.

Once we decide to get over ourselves, we can finally open our eyes to what is happening around us. So, you had a bad experience in church once. Get over yourself. That preacher who tried to console you after your loss was a little pushy. Get over yourself. Get over yourself and realize that Jesus Christ wants, yes wants, and desires to have a personal relationship with each and every one of us.

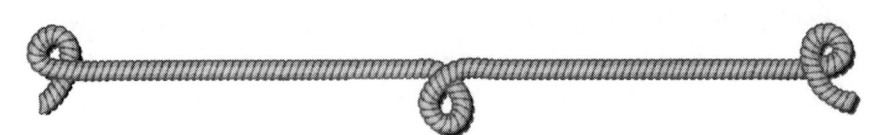

Day 23
"I Need You"

"This day I call the heavens and the earth as witnesses against you that I have set before you life and death, blessings and curses. Now choose life, so that you and your children may live and that you may love the Lord your God, listen to his voice, and hold fast to him. For the Lord is your life, and he will give you many years in the land he swore to give to your fathers, Abraham, Isaac and Jacob" (Deuteronomy 30:19-20 NIV).

"Yet to all who did receive him, to those who believed in his name, he gave the right to become children of God— children born not of natural descent, nor of human decision or a husband's will, but born of God" (John 1:12-13 NIV).

I can remember when my daughter was just turning two-years-old. Almost immediately she went from not talking at all to becoming a chatter box. She began with single words, but very quickly she started stringing words together to form small sentences. The first few weeks she started saying a certain phrase to her mother, and when I got the privilege of hearing her say it to me, oh boy did I melt. When she first wanted to be picked up, she would come up to you, put her hands in the air and say, "I need you." I don't think I have ever heard anything so precious in my life. Of course she just wanted to be picked up, but it really got me to thinking about how much she really does need me. Her mother and I work hard to keep a roof over her head, food on her table and to keep her healthy. We also give her and her brother as much love as we possibly can. However, the real irony behind it is that I need her just as much, or more, than she needs me. She, along with her brother and mother, are my life. I cannot imagine being without them, and they are the reason I do the things I do. So yes, I need her as well. I also got to thinking that this is a whole lot like our relationship with Jesus. Let me frame it for you.

As we have discussed thoroughly, from the very first two people that God put on this earth, He gave them the option to choose. He gave them the option to choose right or wrong, the option to eat the apple or not, and thus the option to have life-everlasting or death. Think about it for a minute because it is a really profound cornerstone of our existence, of Christianity as a whole. I mean look, God could have created us without will, but we would have essentially been robots who did nothing else but worshiped Him all day, every day. But He didn't do that because what would that mean? If someone has the option to choose, and then chooses to love you, it means so much more. It makes the love of that relationship much stronger. Just like in my relationship with my daughter, we all depend on Him for so many things. However, because He gave us the option to choose Him, He essentially "needs" us. "The Maker of heaven and earth does not need us," you say. Oh yeah? What would He fill heaven and earth with without us? Why did He save Lot from Sodom? Why did He save Noah from the flood? Why did He save David from Goliath? Why did He send His only Son, who was blameless, to save us all? Need me to go on? Okay, why will He return again wearing a white robe, riding a white horse to defeat evil once and for all? For us, that's why. Yes, God needs us, just like I need my daughter, and He desires to have a relationship with us exactly like I desire to have a relationship with her.

I think for too long we have tried to have this sterile relationship with God, but He actually wants more. He desires for us to seek Him daily. He desires for us to go to Him with our needs. He desires to have an intimate relationship with us. Do you need the Lord to pick you up and hold you today? I can assure you that He does.

If you still don't believe me. Let's take a look at what He did for us.

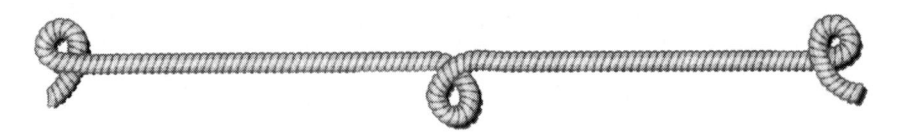

Day 24
"It Is Finished"

"Two other men, both criminals, were also led out with him to be executed. When they came to the place called the Skull, they crucified him there, along with the criminals—one on his right, the other on his left. Jesus said, 'Father, forgive them, for they do not know what they are doing.' And they divided up his clothes by casting lots" (Luke 23:32-34 NIV).

To fully understand the extent that God needs us, I think we must fully comprehend the sacrifice that He made for us. The following is taken from scripture in Matthew 27:27-56 NIV, Mark 15:21-38 NIV, Luke 23:26-49 NIV, and John 19:16-37 NIV, as well as adapted from "The Crucifixion of Jesus Christ" by C. Truman Davis, M.S. March 1965.

The physical trauma of Christ's crucifixion begins when He is in the Garden of Gethsemane. Luke's account says, "And being in agony, He prayed the longer. And His sweat became drops of blood, trickling upon the ground." That is hard for anyone to imagine. I know we have all probably prayed very hard, but to pray and agonize enough that sweat becomes blood is overwhelming. But in fact, there is a rare phenomenon called hemathidrosis, or bloody sweat. Under great emotional stress, tiny capillaries in the sweat glands can break, thus mixing blood with sweat. This process alone could have started to produce marked weakness and possible shock in Him.

After He was arrested in the garden in the middle of the night, Jesus was brought before the Sanhedrin and Caiaphas. While there, a soldier struck Jesus across the face for remaining silent. The palace guards then blindfolded Him and mockingly taunted Him to identify them, and they spat on Him and struck Him in the face.

The next morning, after a likely sleepless night, Jesus—battered, bruised, dehydrated and exhausted—was taken across Jerusalem to meet His fate in front of many of the same mob that welcomed Him into Jerusalem on Palm

Sunday less than a week prior.

Christ was then stripped of His clothing and tied to a post above His head. A Roman legionnaire took a short whip with heavy leather thongs with two small balls of lead attached to the ends of each. The legionnaire lashed Jesus, first with blows that only cut the skin. As the blows continued, they cut deeper, producing oozing blood and then spurting arterial blood. Finally, the skin of His back hung in long ribbons, and the entire area became an unrecognizable mass of torn, bleeding tissue. When it was determined by the centurion in charge that He was near death, the beating stopped.

Jesus was untied and allowed to slump in to a pool of His own blood. Next, they covered Him in a robe and placed a stick in His hand as a makeshift scepter. Mocking Him as the King of Jews, they pressed a crown of thorns into His forehead and took the scepter and struck Him across the head, thus driving the thorns deeper into the flesh of His forehead. The robe, now adhered to His body by coagulated blood, was ripped from His body, causing the wounds to bleed again.

The heavy beam of the cross was tied across his shoulders. Some accounts say it weighed as much as 110lbs. The weight of the beam, coupled with the shock produced by the amount of blood loss, was too much, and He stumbled and fell. The fall caused the rough wood of the beam to gouge into lacerated skin and muscles of His shoulders. He tried to rise again, but couldn't.

When He reached Golgotha, the upright beam was placed on the ground and Jesus was thrown backward with His shoulders against the wood. A legionnaire drove heavy, square, wrought-iron nails through His wrists and into the wood. Next, they placed one foot on the other and drove a single nail through the arch of each foot.

Medical professionals claim that the next events were the worst. Hanging by His arms, trying to catch His breath, Jesus endured hours of limitless pain. As His arms fatigued, great waves of cramps swept over His muscles, knotting them in deep, relentless, throbbing pain. The cramps became so extreme that He became unable to exhale air out of His lungs. Carbon dioxide began to build up in His lungs and blood stream, and His breathing became short and spasmodic. As He struggled to breath, the sack around His heart painfully began to fill with fluid. As his heart became more compressed, it struggled to pump the thick, dehydrated blood through His system. Jesus gasped, "I thirst." A legionnaire raised a sponge full of sour wine to Jesus' parched lips.

After Jesus had received the wine, He said, "It is finished." He bowed His and head and gave up His spirit. As if they had not tortured His body enough, a legionnaire drove a lance through His side into the sack that surrounded His heart, and immediately blood and water poured out.

If I didn't paint a vivid enough picture, watch the movie Passion of the Christ. I sobbed uncontrollably the first time I saw it. Not because of the graphic nature of the film; I cried because of the torture that He endured for my sins. Now, you fathers, remember the account of the last few paragraphs and close your eyes for a second. Let's imagine that you are the last hope for humanity. God comes to you and says, "Eternal life for humanity will not exist unless you give Me your son to die for their sins." Take that in for a minute. Read back over the previous paragraphs. Would you give your son to the horror of crucifixion for your most egregious sins? What about your least egregious sin? What about your neighbor's sin, or the sin of someone you don't know. Picture your son nailed to a cross dying for the people around you. If that's not enough, think of him dying for the sins you have committed yourself. Your God did, and He did that for you.

Are you convicted yet? I certainly am. Now, what point am I trying to make? I have always been raised, as have many of you, that you work for what you get, good or bad. If you work hard, you will be rewarded. If you do bad and don't work hard, you will be punished. And whatever you have created, you live with. That's why I have had such a hard time with the forgiveness of sins. Not with forgiving others, but forgiving myself. As I look back on my life, I can say that I have made my share of mistakes, and seeing that picture of Jesus on the cross just magnifies the guilt I have put on my life because of that. Picturing my own son makes it all that much worse. For many years it was hard for me to accept that Jesus had done that for me and the debt had been paid in full. They were my sins, and I felt that I was supposed to pay for them. Yet, in John 19:30, Jesus said, "It is finished." Which means just that. He gave Himself for the sins of the world, past present and future. Nothing I can do can pay for those sins, but by His grace I am forgiven.

Cowboys, if you have something tearing at you and bringing you down, let go. Do you have things that you have never fully let go of in your life? It could be the sins that you have committed, or maybe even some committed against you. When Jesus died on the cross for all of us, He paid for those sins committed by you and against you. They are remembered no more. You are not worthy and you cannot become worthy enough to pay for your own sins; however, it is only by His grace that our debts are paid. Jesus wants you to let go of them today and live your life with His mercy and grace. He suffered and paid for our sin, so don't diminish His suffering by not accepting His grace. It is finished.

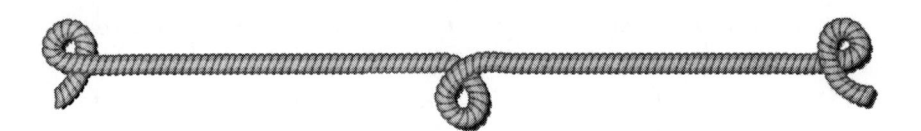

Unit 3

Who We Will Be

Day 25
"Who's Ridin' This Horse?"

"If you declare with your mouth, 'Jesus is Lord,' and believe in your heart that God raised him from the dead, you will be saved. For it is with your heart that you believe and are justified, and it is with your mouth that you profess your faith and are saved. As Scripture says, 'Anyone who believes in him will never be put to shame'" (Romans 10:9-11 NIV).

So, you turned the page. Good, because the last third of this devotional will be about changing your life if you are ready. If not, stash this book in your neighbor's aforementioned feed pickup or continue re-reading Days 1 through 24 until you are ready to change your life. We have spent the last 24 days learning who we are and why we are, and now we will let Him guide us into who we will be.

I am sure that some, if not most of you, are saved, but I am not going to take anything for granted. So, I am going to encourage you to dedicate or rededicate your life to Christ. Here's where most of us get nervous, and most of us get it all wrong. It doesn't have to be a ceremony with pomp and circumstance. You don't necessarily have to go down to the river and dunk yourself, although I do recommend you get baptized if you have not been. The most important thing that you need to do is to recognize you are a sinner, declare that He is Lord and believe in your heart that He was crucified for your sins and raised from the dead, and you will be saved. Just a simple prayer that you say between yourself and the Lord. Some of you will say that you have already done that many years ago in Sunday school or church camp somewhere. That's great, but maybe you have fallen away. Now is a perfect time to rededicate your life to Him. Simply say the prayer, "Jesus, I declare you are Lord. You are Lord of my life, and I believe in my heart that You were crucified for my sins and raised from the dead. I am a sinner, and I want to dedicate my life to You and have You dwell in my heart for eternity." See, that wasn't too hard. I've heard amazing stories of men on the rodeo circuit pulling to the side of the road at night, or others stopping their tractor in the middle of a field, to say a similar prayer.

Okay, so you've said it and you have dedicated your life to Him. Now what? We have to teach ourselves to pray. Remember, He gave us our own free will, and now He is giving us the tools, so who's going to ride this horse that we call life? You are. I want you to consider prayer like all your prized trappings of your trade. Just like your favorite bits and spurs. Prayer is a very useful tool.

Most of us will pray like this, ""Then they cried out to the Lord in their trouble, and he brought them out of their distress" (Psalm 107:28 NIV). I've prayed like this most of my life, and do you know what? It's perfectly okay. Like I have said before, we are His, and He desires to help us. There are going to be times when you are going to need to cry out to Him.

Another thing that I have learned as I've matured in my walk with God is that instead of just screaming for help, it's good to open prayers with praise. "Do not be anxious about anything, but in every situation, by prayer and petition, with thanksgiving, present your requests to God. And the peace of God, which transcends all understanding, will guard your hearts and your minds in Christ Jesus" (Philippians 4:6-7 NIV). We have so many things to be thankful for, but sometimes we lose sight of that for the many pleas and requests we have for God. So, instead try starting prayer with a list of praises, "Lord, I praise You. You are Lord of lords. You are everything to me. I desire to have a relationship with You, and I have these requests of You..."

Sometimes, I hear people say that you shouldn't go to the Lord with requests, but instead you should always pray for God's will in your life. "Father, if you are willing, take this cup from me; yet not my will, but yours be done" (Luke 22:42 NIV). Even Jesus pleaded with God before He was crucified. Now, you know why God didn't grant Jesus' request to do it another way, because salvation couldn't have been done any other way.

So it isn't wrong to make your requests to God, whether they align with His plan or not. Be bold in your prayer requests, get down on your knees and pray fervently to your Father. But keep in mind that God's will and plan is so much more elaborate and incredible than ours. Once we learn that, then we can realize why He created us.

Notes

Day 26
"For You Created Me"

"You have searched me, Lord, and you know me. You know when I sit and when I rise; you perceive my thoughts from afar. You discern my going out and my lying down; you are familiar with all my ways. Before a word is on my tongue you, Lord, know it completely. You hem me in behind and before, and you lay your hand upon me. Such knowledge is too wonderful for me, too lofty for me to attain. Where can I go from your Spirit? Where can I flee from your presence? If I go up to the heavens, you are there; if I make my bed in the depths, you are there. If I rise on the wings of the dawn, if I settle on the far side of the sea, even there your hand will guide me, your right hand will hold me fast. If I say, 'Surely the darkness will hide me and the light become night around me,' even the darkness will not be dark to you; the night will shine like the day, for darkness is as light to you. For you created my inmost being; you knit me together in my mother's womb. I praise you because I am fearfully and wonderfully made; your works are wonderful, I know that full well. My frame was not hidden from you when I was made in the secret place, when I was woven together in the depths of the earth. Your eyes saw my unformed body; all the days ordained for me were written in your book before one of them came to be. How precious to me are your thoughts, God! How vast is the sum of them! Were I to count them, they would outnumber the grains of sand— when I awake, I am still with you" (Psalm 139:1-18 NIV).

It never ceases to amaze me that the Lord created the heavens and the earth, but also took enough time to create me. But He didn't only create me. He took it yet another step. Verse 16 says, "All the days ordained for me were written in your book before one of them came to me." That simple verse there tells me that I was created for a purpose in this life. Think about that for a minute. As God formed you in your mother's womb, He had a meticulous plan for what your life would be. The funny and all too ironic thing about God creating us this way is that He too often also gives us traits and qualities that end up humbling us. Let me explain.

I'm a planner. It's what I do. I like to have a clear, concise plan for the task ahead, and I like to implement that plan as closely as I can. I'm definitely not inflexible, but it puts my mind at ease to have a meticulous plan going into whatever task or endeavor I'm entering. Here's where the irony comes into play. A lot of times I think I'm bold enough to set out a plan for my life, only to find out that the Lord wanted me to go in a different direction. I've even shouted, "That's not the plan Lord." Yet, in His wisdom, He calmly guides me toward the "real" plan. I truly believe that God does not reveal everything to us because we would simply take our plan and run. In other words, without knowing the future and the specific plan for our lives, we have to rely on God for His guidance and remain in Him for prayer and petition. Over and over in my life I am starting to realize that His plan is more perfect that I could ever imagine for myself. Go back to verse 6, which reads, "Such knowledge is too wonderful for me, too lofty for me to attain." I trust Him, and I trust that His plan for my life is much better than I could have ever dreamed.

Now, are you feeling good about yourself? Well, don't get mad at me because I'm not going to tell you that life is going to be easy after you have decided to live for the Lord. From now on in life you are going to ride through deep valleys at times, and other times you will ride on the tops of mountains. Just remember, that grass (spiritual growth) always grows deeper in the valleys of life. And you're going to need that grass because things might get tough. But He will always be beside you, and He will carry you if necessary. Commit yourself to His plan. Ask and seek guidance, and He will never leave your side. His promise is profound and faithful because you will need Him.

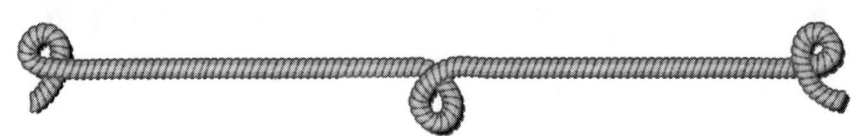

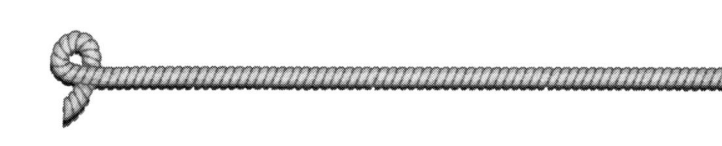

Day 27
"Things Might Get Tough"

" 'I have told you these things, so that in me you may have peace. In this world you will have trouble. But take heart! I have overcome the world' " (John 16:33 NIV).

It was January 2013 and I backed in the roping box with JB Miller at the Fort Worth Livestock Show Ranch Rodeo. Fort Worth is always my favorite rodeo of the year because of its history and nostalgia. Opposite of us, in the other box, was Kye Fuston. We were the three that were designated to go in the double mugging. Our strategy was for Kye to rope the yearling, and JB, who is also about my size, and I were to mug and tie the yearling. The chute cracked and Kye roped him like Tuff Cooper. However, what happened next was not quite as pretty. When the big, Charolais yearling hit the end of the line he came back at us and worked JB and me over and over and over until we finally got him mugged and tied. In the process of mugging him, he stepped right in the middle of my back.

I didn't think much of it as I thought I simply had a muscle bruise. I went to the local doctors a couple times and tried a chiropractor, but nothing really seemed to help much. One morning in the middle of March, however, the pain came to a head. I had awoke early because I couldn't sleep and decided to come to the living room. I tried laying on the couch when it intensified. A pain shot through my back like I had never felt before, and it caused me to scream and fall flat to the floor. I just lay there motionless for a few moments and the pain started to lessen, so I decided that I would try to take a hot shower. Once I got in the shower, the pain came back. I screamed again and almost fainted. Cara came running into the bathroom and asked what was wrong. I explained very simply, "You have to get me somewhere."

Cara and I have a little pact that we don't go to the local emergency rooms, but I was in so much pain that I told her that we should probably go through Tucumcari on our way to Amarillo in case I had to stop. However, the awkward thing was that once we got to Tucumcari my pain had started to subside. So, we called my private care provider in Amarillo and made a routine appointment. By the time we got to Dr. Clark's office, I was walking and feeling fine, but he insisted that we take a CT scan just in case. Let me paint the picture for you a little. Grady was 2 and a half years old, and Cara was 9 months pregnant with Josey. So, from the time I took the scan until he read the results, Cara had taken Grady out of the waiting room to play. As I sat there in the waiting room, I thought to myself, "I sure hope that these kidney stones don't keep me away from work too long." We were in preparation to start branding, and I sure had a lot on my mind. I'll never forget the moment when Dr. Clark came back in the room. He simply said, "Kris, you have a mass on your left kidney, and we need to get it looked at very soon." The room started to spin. "What do you mean a mass," I thought? "What's the medical definition of a mass?" I wondered. I asked simply, "What is it?" He gave me his best medical school answer, "I think it's a tumor, but I cannot be for sure." You see, what had happened was that when the Charolais calf stepped in my back, it aggravated the tumor and made it start bleeding. More than likely, that was the reason it was found at all.

I walked out to the waiting room, and Cara asked what I had found out. I didn't want to make a scene in the doctor's office, so I told her I would tell her in the car. When we loaded Grady in the car, and my wife and unborn daughter slid into the front seat beside me, tears streamed down my face and I uttered the words that would literally change our family's life forever: "They think I've got cancer."

There comes a pivotal moment in your life when you really get to find out what you are made of. I just wasn't ready. I was still a mere infant in Christ.

Day 28
"A Worldly Solution?"

"Brothers and sisters, I could not address you as people who live by the Spirit but as people who are still worldly—mere infants in Christ. I gave you milk, not solid food, for you were not yet ready for it. Indeed, you are still not ready" (1 Corinthians 3:1-2 NIV).

I visited a specialist a week later, and he confirmed our greatest fears, and our rug was pulled completely out from under us. The most complicating part of it all was that the appointment with the specialist was a day before Cara was scheduled to have Josey. I was scared to death that the stress would induce Cara, so I had her stay in town the whole week before she was scheduled for a Caesarean section. Fortunately my mom and sister accompanied me to the appointment. You might be thinking where God was in all this, and how was my faith. I had been saved for about 20 years and considered myself a strong Christian for the last 12 to 15 years. God was undoubtedly in our prayers and thoughts constantly, but the next few weeks were a complete blur. In that time, we witnessed the birth of our beautiful daughter, and my condition worsened by the day.

Finally, upset with the lack of urgency of my first specialist, we found a specialist in Lubbock that would see us. Cara's mother, father and sister were at the ranch with us, helping Cara recover and visiting our new addition. I had been feeling better right before my appointment in Lubbock, and my mother was going to meet me there, so I suggested that I drive myself. Cara's dad intervened, and I am glad he did. The drive to Lubbock that day seemed to aggravate my kidney. By the time I arrived at the doctor's office, I was in obvious pain. The doctor saw me and decided that we should take my kidney out within the week. I was relieved because that was a lot sooner than the other specialist had suggested, but as I sat with the assistant to schedule surgery, tears began to run down my face.

The next few hours were a time in my life I would like to soon forget. I nearly collapsed in the doctor's office, and my mom and father-in-law rushed me a couple blocks away to the hospital. As my doctor wrote the admittance papers, I lay on my side in the waiting room groaning with pain. After what seemed like hours, I was taken up to the urology wing on the sixth floor, and although no one knew my name, they knew exactly who I was because I had been screaming at the top of my lungs. For the next couple hours, I wretched and screamed in pain. The nurses quickly found out that I was allergic to morphine, as it seemed to only intensify the pain, and hospital bureaucracy couldn't seem to find a solution quickly enough. As I lay there gripping my mother's hand and puking in the trash can, the pain was so intense that I prayed to God to just take me right then and there. The last thing I remember before falling asleep was the feeling as though I was floating three feet off the bed from all the narcotics they finally administered.

I had a young family, my whole life in front of me, and now I was faced with uncertainty. The next morning I was quickly rushed into major surgery, and I can assure you that I was very scared. I had a lot of encouragement, and a lot of people said, "Don't lose hope." They repeated, "Don't give up." "Sure," I would say. No problem. I mean, lots of people get cancer and come through it. I would read that a lot of people would lose a kidney and go on to live a normal life. So, I said I was okay.

But in reality, I didn't know how to hope. I was leaning on a worldly solution to my problem. I prayed and I hoped, but I wasn't ready to give the entire situation to Him because I believed modern medicine was the light at the end of my tunnel.

After my kidney and the tumor were removed, I read every study and report about my diagnosis that I could, and I learned that because of the early stage of the tumor, I had a good statistical chance of remaining cancer free. That was good news because I was busy and had important things to do. Although my recovery was slow, I quickly returned to my former life—consumed by my profession and caught up in the things of this world.

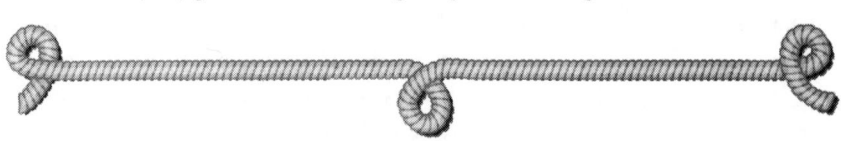

Day 29
"Gut Check"

"Do you not know? Have you not heard? The Lord is the everlasting God, the Creator of the ends of the earth. He will not grow tired or weary, and his understanding no one can fathom. He gives strength to the weary and increases the power of the weak. Even youths grow tired and weary, and young men stumble and fall; but those who hope in the Lord will renew their strength. They will soar on wings like eagles; they will run and not grow weary, they will walk and not be faint" (Isaiah 40:28-31 NIV).

    For some of you who have been through trials, you might understand how I really didn't know how to hope. Of course I had faith and had "hoped" for other things. But my true hope was still in its infancy. I had always been a doer. I had worked very hard to put myself in a position to be successful in school and in my career, and while the Lord had blessed me very much, I felt like my work ethic had pulled me through. I had hoped that God would bring me a Proverbs 31 wife, and He did. We both hoped that we would be able to start a family, and we did. With each step of the way we had stayed grounded in the Lord and went to Him in prayer. However, something was different this time. Something was missing. It wasn't as though God was silent in the time after my surgery, but it was almost as though we didn't lean on Him entirely. In the back of my mind was the fact that only 30 to 40 percent of people with my diagnosis have a recurrence of cancer. So this seemed like a minor bump in the road, and I was ready to get back to my life.
    Almost exactly one year after my surgery, I had a routine CT scan. I got a frantic call from my doctor, saying he had found that the cancer had moved into my lungs and on my right adrenal gland. I also learned a couple weeks later that it had moved into a bone in my right foot. Whatever confidence or hope I had built up during the past 12 months, it was all taken away in a couple weeks' time. That light at the end of the tunnel got a whole lot dimmer.

It was during the next few months that I actually began to ask myself what I was really made of. Worldly statistics told me that I had a 7 percent chance to live within the next five years. One doctor told me that because the cancer had metastasized to bone, I had 18 months to live. This was the pivotal moment in my life. I could decide to pack it up and feel sorry for myself, or I could decide to do something very different. You really never know how strong you are until being strong is the only choice you have.

It was in this time that I had no other choice but to start giving it all to Christ, and the more I gave it to Him the more He started working on me. Unbeknownst to me, He had actually been working on me and preparing me for this. In the months prior to learning that I had stage 4 cancer, a lot of things were happening in my life. My wife and a good friend of ours insisted that I go on a Walk to Emmaus. I had never been before, and I felt like I really didn't have the time to go. It was, however, a three-day event that changed my life forever. I had also been convicted to begin teaching the Gospel again. When I was a professor at Texas Tech I had led a Bible study for some of the students.

So, I had a gut check decision to make. I could decide to feel sorry for myself, or I could get over myself and figure out how to use my situation to witness to others. Quickly, the Lord put an idea in my head to start a Bible study on Facebook. We live out in the middle of nowhere, but that didn't mean that I couldn't share with my friends and family how God was working in my life. So there it began. Cara and I named it Western Faithbook and decided I would post my first study right away.

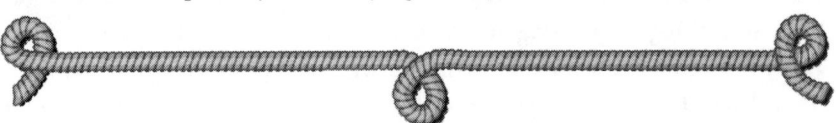

Day 30
"Harden Your Hope"

"Therefore, since we have been justified through faith, we have peace with God through our Lord Jesus Christ, through whom we have gained access by faith into this grace in which we now stand. And we boast in the hope of the glory of God. Not only so, but we also glory in our sufferings, because we know that suffering produces perseverance; perseverance, character; and character, hope. And hope does not put us to shame, because God's love has been poured out into our hearts through the Holy Spirit, who has been given to us" (Romans 5:1-5 NIV).

The second week into my Western Faithbook study was really a turning point for me. I'd had surgery on my right foot, and again the doctors had a hard time with my pain control, so they subsequently overmedicated me. The two bones in my right foot were removed and replaced with bone cement. Every time I began to fall asleep in my hospital bed, I wound up biting my tongue due to the heavy amount of pain medication. I gave up on sleeping and opened my Bible to the verses above.

As I reread the scripture over and over, verses 3–4 jumped off the page at me. "Not only so, but we also glory in our sufferings, because we know suffering produces perseverance; perseverance, character; and character, hope" (Romans 5:3-4 NIV). You see, I had no idea how to hope. My hope was in its infancy because it had never really been tried. I had never really gone through the type of suffering that would produce perseverance, which would produce character, which would in turn produce hope—the kind of hope that would get me through what I was going to face. I spent the next couple hours reading in Romans and found the following scripture as well. "For in this hope we were saved. But hope that is seen is no hope at all. Who hopes for what they already have? But if we hope for what we do not yet have, we wait for it patiently" (Romans 8:24-25 NIV).

Instantaneously, the Lord started sending me blessings, and teaching me things that I believe He never could have taught me without this trial. For example, we were sitting at breakfast one morning before my pre-op appointment. I looked over to the right of me and a family was sitting with a young boy that was about 10 years old. He was bald from chemo treatments, emaciated and obviously had gone through a lot of torment. While in the pre-op room waiting for anesthesia, there was a 3-year-old girl to the right of me, and a man to my left that was about to have his kidney taken out. I went to my Lord in prayer right there and said, "Lord, thank you that my kids are not the ones affected by this terrible disease, and thank you that I am not getting my kidney removed today (I had already been through that horrible experience), and I lift up these people around me in prayer." I found myself not worrying about my predicament, but praying for the people who had not found the peace that I had.

Since my diagnosis, my life has rocked along up and down with a lot of hopeful moments and a ton of heartbreaks. It has seemed that every time I could see a little light at the end of the tunnel, another setback darkened it. In true hardship, however, my hope has become a strength. See, each time my hope was damaged, it was forced to come back stronger. Each time I had to dig deeper to find a stronger version of my previous hope. At one point, I had to take multiple painkillers a day to walk on my right foot. The pain was excruciating, and my orthopedic surgeon suggested that amputation was my only choice. I can tell you that my hope took a blow. However, a few months later I was off 95 percent of my painkillers.

Every time I have received good news about my progress, I can assure you that I am extremely hopeful that it becomes a new plateau for me. However, I am not going to harden my heart. I am going to harden my hope. I'm going to harden it so much that if I need to dig deep, it will come through for me again. See, I've come to realize that hope is not an every-once-in-a-while thing. Hope is an all-the-time thing.

Cowboys, not one person will read this who doesn't have something going on in their life, or the lives of their loved ones, who doesn't need a good dose of hope. Let me assure you, no matter how bad it gets, you shouldn't abandon your hope. Don't allow yourself to give up. You may just think you need your hope now. But the Lord may be strengthening your hope for when you really need it. Don't harden your heart. Harden your hope.

Day 31
"Listen, Obey, and Rejoice"

"As for everyone who comes to me and hears my words and puts them into practice, I will show you what they are like. They are like a man building a house, who dug down deep and laid the foundation on rock. When a flood came, the torrent struck that house but could not shake it, because it was well built. But the one who hears my words and does not put them into practice is like a man who built a house on the ground without a foundation. The moment the torrent struck that house, it collapsed and its destruction was complete" (Luke 6:47-49 NIV).

Listen, I didn't spend several days sharing my trial and testimony to bring attention to me. I did it to give you a roadmap for when you have troubles in this life, and it's likely you will. When I first started learning about going through a trial, I read that I would learn to rejoice in my tribulation, but I never really believed it. I thought, "How could someone learn to rejoice in pain, anguish and suffering?" I have learned that there are three distinct actions that you must take through a trial: listen, obey and rejoice. Let me walk you through it.

During this trial, my emotions have really run the spectrum from hope to despair, from fight to surrender. My health has gone from flickers of hope to downright hopelessness. Yet, never in my life have I been as connected with the Lord as I have been in the past couple years, because I finally decided to listen to Him. I have truly been still, listened, and He has spoken to me numerous times in the spirit with phrases like, "Be obedient, and I'll do my part; the act of healing is manifest in the proclamation of your faith; a prayer prayed does not go devoid," and many others. Verse 47 above starts, "As for everyone who comes to me and hears my words and puts them into practice, I will show you what they are like." The verse goes on to say that by listening you can strengthen the foundation of your life.

So after I started listening, I began to obey. And by obeying He started making some much-needed changes in my life. First, during this time my wife and I have spent a lot of time together, and He has used that strengthen our relationship with each other and jointly with Him. I tell her daily, "I have never loved you more," and I can honestly say that my love for her grows deeper every single day. He also showed me that I needed to slow down and put my family in front of my career. By doing that, He would still bless my career, but missed time with my family is something that I could never get back. And by obeying Him, I now truly mean it when I say that I have learned to rejoice in my tribulation, knowing that it will bring much-needed perseverance for the much harder days to come. I know that perseverance will bring character, and character will in turn bring hope. And what else do you have in some situations, besides hope?

One day I was having a casual conversation with someone when they asked me if I wished that I had experienced complete healing before my kidney had been removed and then metastasized a year later. I quickly said, "You bet!" But that response haunted me the rest of the day. Finally, that night I realized that I did not wish that I had been healed immediately from cancer because it has taken this tribulation to make me a better Christian, husband, father and man. This is a bold statement, but I would not give that up for anything. Look guys, I don't know if I'll ever be on the backside of this or not. I have faith that I will, but only God knows. Sometimes I guess when you are as stubborn as I am, it takes a big bump in the road to realize what He has laid before you. God has given me so many blessings in my life, from the best family I could ever ask for to the coolest job on the planet. Cowboys, don't take for granted anything that happens in your life. Please just listen, obey and rejoice in the outcome.

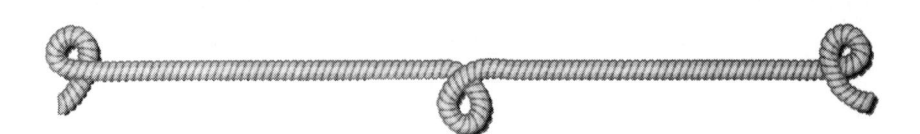

Day 32
"His Promise To Fight For Us"

"At that time I commanded Joshua: 'You have seen with your own eyes all that the Lord your God has done to these two kings. The Lord will do the same to all the kingdoms over there where you are going. Do not be afraid of them; the Lord your God himself will fight for you'" (Deuteronomy 3:21-22 NIV).

In the above passage, Moses was in the process of turning over the leadership of the Jewish people to Joshua, and there were still very powerful and formidable challenges ahead of Joshua. Moses reiterated God's promise to personally fight for Joshua and His people. If you have someone to fight for you and with you, then what else do you really need in life? Let me frame it for you.

We've all got that one friend, right? The one you don't mind stepping into a sticky situation with. Whether you are in a spot you shouldn't be or just need help getting out of a bind, that person is going to be there ready to fight and get you out of there. It always puts my mind at ease knowing I have that kind of friend.

Now, Jesus' sacrifice on the cross has guaranteed life everlasting. But, His promise goes further than that because we still live in this world. Just as important as His life-everlasting commitment to us cowboys is His promise to fight for us, here and now. His back will be against ours, fists raised, ready to help us out of our problems.

Have I lost you yet? See, after you are saved, everything changes. Before, the fight was with Him. Yes, with Him. Hang with me for a bit. "Whoever is not with me is against me, and whoever does not gather with me scatters" (Matthew 12:30 NIV). But now you have dedicated your life to Him, and He has done the same to you. Until we are united with Him in heaven, we live in this world, and it can be a rough and nasty place. Now, instead of struggling against Him, the struggle is still in this world, but the big change is that you have the Most High God in your corner.

Are you going to need Him to fight for you in this life? Just look around for a minute. If you don't, then you are a lot tougher I am. Sometimes it gets overwhelming for me, especially when I see the amount of evil there is in the world. Every time I hear of a parent losing a child, or a child contracting a debilitating disease, it makes me question the purpose of it all. "For our struggle is not against flesh and blood, but against the rulers, against the authorities, against the powers of this dark world and against the spiritual forces of evil in the heavenly realms" (Ephesians 6:12 NIV). The sooner we recognize that we are in a battle, the sooner we can pick a side and be ready to fight. Satan is a real and formidable enemy. "The thief comes only to steal and kill and destroy;" (John 10:10 NIV). Oh, and in case you haven't read to the end of the story, God wins.

I love hearing heartfelt testimonies from people who have been in life's trenches and had the Lord by their side. Absolutely incredible and simply miraculous things are put into motion because of His willingness to fight for us. It also gives me solace knowing the amount of power that He is willing to bring to a fight. "I pray that they eyes of your heart may be enlightened in order that you may know the hope to which he has called you, the riches of his glorious inheritance in his holy people, and his incomparably great power for us who believe. That power is the same as the mighty strength he exerted when he raised Christ from the dead and seated him at his right hand in the heavenly realms," (Ephesians 1:18-20 NIV).

Yes, cowboys He will fight for you, and He will use the same strength that He used to resurrect Christ. That's good enough for me.

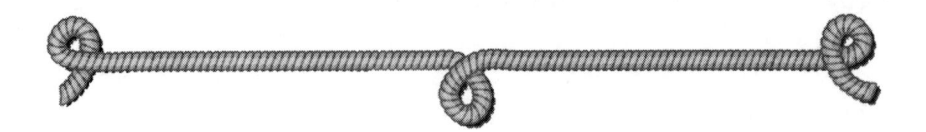

Day 33
"The Six Things That Really Matter"

"But seek first his kingdom and his righteousness, and all these things will be given to you as well" (Matthew 6:33 NIV).

I used to think that another win at a horseshow or a ranch rodeo really mattered, or maybe a really cool new pair of spurs. But during the last few years, the Lord showed me the six things that really matter in my life, and I wanted to share them with you. Hopefully they are some of the things that really matter in your life.

I know this one sounds cliché, but the first thing is to pick something that you love to do, and you will never work a day in your life. I have been blessed enough to live this one, twice. "Delight yourself in the Lord, and He shall give you the desires of your heart" (Psalms 37:4 NIV). My first dream was to be college professor, and I became one. But, how does a college professor go to work on a ranch? You pray about it! My wife and I started an eight month journey of prayer and daily communion while I was an assistant professor, asking the Lord to open doors and "give me the desires of my heart." And He certainly gave them to me. In 2009, to the bewilderment of many I quit my well-paying job at Texas Tech University and took a job at Matador Ranch in Matador, Texas. It was probably the best time of Cara's and my life! Then, in a little over a year, there was an opportunity to manage one of the most storied ranches in the world, the Bell Ranch. I applied for it, and with much prayer and faith, I was given the job.

The second thing I've learned that really matters is forgiving easily and often. "Therefore as the elect of God, holy and beloved, put on tender mercies, kindness, humility, meekness, longsuffering, bearing with one another, and forgiving one another, if anyone has a complaint against another; even as Christ forgave you, so you also must do" (Colossians 3:12–13, NKJV). What if we learned to walk our everyday lives living like Jesus and forgiving people as soon as they have committed a transgression against us? How much more productive and enjoyable would work be if you forgave people like that? I'm not saying that I don't still get angry or frustrated, but I have really been working on this one in my life. Forgive and let go, and your life will be enriched by it.

The third thing that I have found that really matters is to honor the people around you. "Honor all people. Love the brotherhood. Fear God. Honor the king" (1 Peter 2:17 NKJV). I have always had a really easy time honoring the people who are closest to me. It's easy to honor my mother and father, my wife and kids. It's even easy to honor my grandparents, uncles and aunts, and Cara's family as well. I've had an easy time also honoring the people that I work closely with, many of whom are my closest friends. I have, however, had a hard time honoring people whom I don't know well or make an uneasy first impression on me. Will Rogers once said, "I never met a man I didn't like." Well, I'm going to be honest. I've met several I didn't like, but God's word says, "Honor all people." The Lord has really been doing a work in me on this one in the past few years. I'm big on first impressions, and like it or not the first impression someone gives me is generally how I remember them. However, lately I have been learning to see Christ's creation in every person. You see, Christ created everyone, so there is a good work in every person you meet. It's my job to find that in each person.

The fourth thing that I have found that really matters is to do all things with integrity. "The righteous man walks in his integrity; his children are blessed after him" (Proverbs 20:7 NKJV). This has always been very important to me, largely because I have learned from the example of some men with a lot of integrity. Once I was speaking with my farrier when I lived in College Station, and we were speaking about my father, and I was lamenting about how my dad sometimes lets his clients get the best of him on deals. Shon, being older and wiser than I was, said, "That may be so, but I have never heard anyone in the horse industry say the Earnest Wilson got the best of them." That really resonated with me. Saddles and trophies fade, but a man's integrity is attached to him for perpetuity.

The fifth thing that really matters is to not be afraid to fail. Let me take you back to my story about the desires of my heart. When I was called about the job for the Bell Ranch, my first inclination was to decline the job. Besides, I had only been seriously doing this ranching thing for a little over a year, and I had never employed anyone. However, I prayed about it and followed the doors that my Lord opened. Lord, did I ever make some mistakes. But I can honestly say that the Lord has done a good work in me. A lot of it has come from some good colleagues in Silver Spur Ranches (which owns the Bell) and the absolute best crew on the planet. When I first came to the Bell, the joke around was that I was the "kid from Texas." How was this kid going to manage this historic ranch? I have had the pleasure of driving some those critics around the ranch in the past year or two. That has been fun. As Theodore Roosevelt said, "If he fails, at least he fails while daring greatly; so that his place shall never be with those cold and timid souls, who neither know victory nor defeat."

The sixth and most important thing that really matters is to find a personal relationship with Christ Jesus. "Jesus said to him, 'I am the way, the truth, and the life. No one comes to the Father except through Me' " (John 14:6 NKJV). I have found that after I found a personal relationship with Christ, my life is truly fulfilled. Seek Him and He will order your steps. Follow Him and He will align your life.

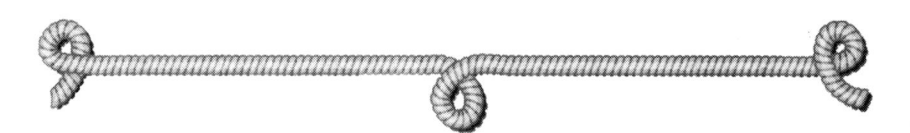

Notes

Day 34
"In His Time"

"He has made everything beautiful in its time. He has also set eternity in the human heart; yet no one can fathom what God has done from beginning to end" (Ecclesiastes 3:11 NIV).

If you've worked cattle very long, you've heard the saying, "slow is fast." You probably first heard it as a young cowpuncher, and it may have taken a while to come around to it, but it's definitely true. You realize that if sometimes you let things happen, instead of trying to make them happen, then everything runs a lot smoother. The funny thing is that God works the exact same way. Let me tell you a story about how I know.

It's inevitable and it has undoubtedly happened to you over and over. Once you get saved and start living your life for Jesus, you have an undeniable urge to share your experience with those around you, especially those who might not be saved. You know you are going to heaven, and you want those closest to you to go as well. But a lot of times the people who are closest to you are the hardest to witness to. I found myself in this situation with my father several years ago. My dad is my hero, and he has always been. So, how do you talk to your hero about Jesus, being saved and going to heaven? My dad was raised in a Christian home by a strong Christian mother, but in my 30 years or so of living at the time, we had never had a conversation about his salvation, and I had no idea how to start.

One Sunday morning while we were both at a ranch horse sale in San Antonio, Texas, I decided it was time for me to make my move. Steve Friskup had just given an early morning service and had offered to visit with anyone who had something on their mind that morning. Dad and I were both horseback, and while he started to warm his horse up, I doubled back across the arena to catch Steve. We both had known Steve for a long time, and I thought it was best for Steve and I to grab Dad that morning and make sure he was right with Jesus. See where I am going with this? I had identified help, and I thought we could corner Dad, run him through the chute and slap some Jesus on him. My plan was probably going to work like it would with a set of old cows who didn't want to be palpated that day. I finally got to Steve and explained my plan in full. Steve pulled me aside and said, "Let's do this another way. Let's pray that Jesus starts a work in your dad's life and he shows him in His time." We prayed, but to be quite honest I was disappointed. I had lost a lot of sleep over this issue, and I wished it to be remedied a lot quicker than that.

As it turns out, His time was perfect. On the following Tuesday, my grandmother was hospitalized. I was back home in Lubbock, and I was the first relative to get to New Mexico to see her. I immediately called Dad, explained the severity of her situation, and told him he needed to fly in. As it turns out, my grandmother passed away that week, and I was able to be there with my dad to console and witness to him. It didn't take any big speeches or productions, and it definitely wasn't fast. But, being there and showing him how Jesus helped me grieve was enough to make him consider his own salvation. The next Sunday, exactly one week since I had spoken to Steve about Dad, we stopped at Steve's church on the way home and Dad pledged his life to Jesus and was baptized.

Cowboys, His time is perfect time. A lot of people have had a bad experience with church or been condemned by family members or others who claim to be more righteous. Pushing Jesus on someone like that likely will drive them away. Sometimes letting things happen instead of trying to make them happen makes everything run smoother. Yes, slow is fast.

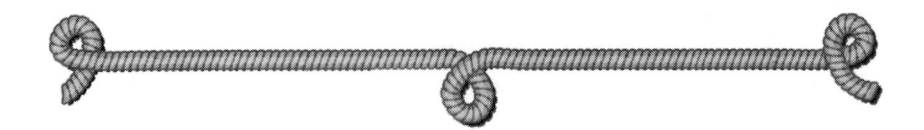

Day 35
"The Thorn In My Side"

"Even if I should choose to boast, I would not be a fool, because I would be speaking the truth. But I refrain, so no one will think more of me than is warranted by what I do or say, or because of these surpassingly great revelations. Therefore, in order to keep me from becoming conceited, I was given a thorn in my flesh, a messenger of Satan, to torment me. Three times I pleaded with the Lord to take it away from me. But he said to me, 'My grace is sufficient for you, for my power is made perfect in weakness.' Therefore I will boast all the more gladly about my weaknesses, so that Christ's power may rest on me. That is why, for Christ's sake, I delight in weaknesses, in insults, in hardships, in persecutions, in difficulties. For when I am weak, then I am strong" (2 Corinthians 12:6–10 NIV).

I think sometimes in my Christian walk I get frustrated because I just can't get ahead. It's because of the stumbling block, or thorn in my side. But the irony behind it is that it's exactly what I need. Let me try to frame it for you.

The Apostle Paul begins chapter 12 in 2 Corinthians by telling the Corinthians about his visions and revelations; however, he is quick to also tell them about the thorn that was put in his side. The thorn was intended to be a beneficial thing to Paul to keep him from being conceited because of his ability to foresee visions and revelations. Theologians have argued for many years about what exactly Paul's thorn was. Obviously, in this instance and ours for that matter, Paul's thorn is some sort of stumbling block that keeps him humble and continuing to seek the Lord for help. Some say that Paul's thorn is his arrogance, or even his guilt from what he was before he was saved by the Lord. Others say that Paul may have dealt with temptation or depression. Still others insist that Paul was affected by a physical ailment that kept him in constant check.

When you think about it, God's metaphor of a thorn is so befitting not just to Paul, but to our lives as well. In the passage above, Paul explains that his thorn came to him by way of a messenger of Satan. I think we have all had the displeasure of having a thorn stuck in us. Sometimes the more you poke and prod at it, the worse it gets. Paul's displeasure of the thorn is apparent because of his pleas with God to take it from him. I have to believe that after all Paul endured that his pleas to God are probably not to be taken lightly. The irony behind this whole story is that the thorn is obviously from Satan, but allowed by God to benefit Paul. Let me say that again. God allowed Paul to be tormented so that he would become a better person, and more importantly remain a better person, by continually seeking Him because, "My grace is sufficient for you, for my power is made perfect in weakness." Does that remind you of anyone? Reminds me of me. Why is our human nature so lazy, or vile, or plain sinful, that we cannot trust ourselves to simply be good on our own, or seek Him without having to be constantly prodded by some thorn?

Let me ask you, do you have any thorns in your side? Sometimes I feel like I've busted through a mesquite thicket after some ol' wild cow and forgot to put my leggings on. You? Ever felt that way? Sometimes I think, "Am I so slow that the Lord has to put several thorns in my side to keep me seeking him?" Reviewing this passage is good for us because we are reminded that even after everything Paul did, he still struggled. I mean, think about it for a second. Paul penned a large part of the New Testament, started some of the first and most influential churches in history, and was a key figure in the spread of Christianity. Pretty powerful things for the kingdom of God, huh? Yet, God felt that if He didn't allow a thorn in Paul's side, that his human nature would taint all the good he was performing in the world. Paul was a man who undoubtedly sought God, yet he too needed help. He too needed God's grace. So, next time you feel that thorn dig in a little in your side, dab a lot of God's grace on it.

Day 36
"Your Greatest Test"

"This righteousness is given through faith in Jesus Christ to all who believe. There is no difference between Jew and Gentile, for all have sinned and fall short of the glory of God, and all are justified freely by his grace through the redemption that came by Christ Jesus" (Romans 3:22–24 NIV).

"But because of his great love for us, God, who is rich in mercy, made us alive with Christ even when we were dead in transgressions—it is by grace you have been saved" (Ephesians 2:4–5 NIV).

Remember Day 18, "The Question That Haunts Us All"? Well the question was basically, do I have what it takes, or am I good enough? We spend most of our lives trying to answer that question and proving ourselves to the people around us. What if I told you that you aren't good enough and you don't have what it takes, and neither do I? You might say that I duped you and would probably stop reading this devotional. Give me a minute to explain.

Cowboys by definition are free-spirited, untamed souls who at the very core of their being are resistant to being tied to anything, much less Christianity. That independent nature also makes it tough for cowboys to admit that they need Jesus. But, the most hindering trait that makes an ordinary man a good cowboy but a poor Christian is pride in his self-reliance. See, most cowboys want to own their actions, good or bad. If something goes wrong, a good cowboy will step up and take blame for it. If something goes right, he will be less apt to claim it, but make no mistake that he takes pride in the accomplishment. It's a sense of self-reliance and independence that drives us. So, by the very nature of being a cowboy, men are very reluctant to accept God's grace because they did not earn it. In their mind they say, "I am so sorry and have done so many things wrong in my life, there is no way I am going to show myself inside the doors of that church." So they remain lost.

God's grace, however, is defined as the love and mercy given to us by God because God desires us to have it, not because of anything we have done to earn it. See, God loves us unconditionally. He loves us regardless of what we have done and regardless of what we ever do. So, to say or feel like you are unworthy of being in the presence of God doesn't matter. We are and will always be unworthy; however, there is nothing that you or I have ever done that can separate or weaken His love for us. Now, because He loves us so much, He sent us His only Son to take our sin on Himself, and that's God's grace. Although we never earned it, God's grace is a gift and we must accept that gift or perish.

So, your greatest test in this life is to realize the true answer to the question that has haunted you. You do not have what it takes, and you are not good enough. It's tough, I know, because I have struggled with it for many years and still struggle with it. Like you, I want to own my actions. And somehow, even though it's a corrupt concept, if you can't own your actions then you don't want to accept His grace. So to pass the test, you have to put your accomplishments—good and bad—aside. You have to put aside your wanting to own your actions. You have to put your put your pride and selfishness aside to realize that it's really all about you. Yes, let me say that again. It's all about you. Christ died for you. Once you realize and accept the one gift that you can never repay, you will have passed your greatest test.

Day 37
"Look Around"

"Praise the Lord. Praise the Lord from the heavens; praise him in the heights above. Praise him, all his angels; praise him, all his heavenly hosts. Praise him, sun and moon; praise him, all you shining stars. Praise him, you highest heavens and you waters above the skies. Let them praise the name of the Lord, for at his command they were created, and he established them for ever and ever— he issued a decree that will never pass away" (Psalm 148:1-6 NIV).

"For since the creation of the world God's invisible qualities—his eternal power and divine nature—have been clearly seen, being understood from what has been made, so that people are without excuse"
(Romans 1:20 NIV).

Can you see God in what you do? Now, I'm not talking about the works in your life. Rather, I'm talking about can you see God in the everyday happenings at your ranch or in your occupation? If not, I would encourage you to look around.

What about that hay crop you just toiled to bring in from the field? Think God didn't have anything to do with that? He provided the nutrients from His earth, provided the sunlight from His light and watered it in His timing. What about those big calves you have been seeing this fall? Who helped you keep them alive during that bad snow storm last spring? Who provides you with the most beautiful country to ride through in the morning, and just who do you think paints those gorgeous sunsets? Who kept that colt from landing on you squarely when he flipped over last spring, and who brought your family home safely in the snowstorm last winter?

If there was ever a doubt in your mind about God, all you should have to do is look around. We have what we have and we are who we are because He blesses us. If we humble ourselves to Him and allow Him to bless us, then He will bless us beyond our wildest dreams.

One of my favorite things to do on the ranch is to praise Him while we are jigging out in the morning. Most people like to rope and drag calves, and I'm no exception, but the gather in the morning is my favorite part of the day. I like commuting and communing with the crew as we trot along, but I also like to raise my hands in the air and praise Him when I get by myself. It's a time of reflection and prayer that I cannot explain. I made a promise to myself that if He would give me the desires of my heart, I would praise Him each and every morning for it, and jigging out in the dark, to ride into a beautiful sunrise has to be God's most beautiful cathedral.

I missed both the 2013 and 2014 branding seasons because of surgery. Oh, I was around, but horseback wasn't an option either time. In 2015, however, I started to feel pretty good right about the time branding started. We were camped at the Roundtop Pens and needed to trot to the back of Seco Breeding Trap. It's about a six- or seven-mile trot. We left early, before sunrise, and Zack asked me to lead the crew. I had led many drives in my life, but none so special. I hadn't led a drive in over two years and I was excited to be horseback again. As we trotted along I noticed every beautiful thing that God had created, from the green on the mesquite leaves to the blooms on the cholla. I admired the beads of sweat that rolled along the sides of my horse's neck and the stiff reins in my hand. The best part, however, was after I dropped Zack off. I trotted to a little hill on the back side of the trap, raised my hands in the air and just praised Him. My bank account hadn't changed, but I was the richest man in the world that morning. All I had to do was look around.

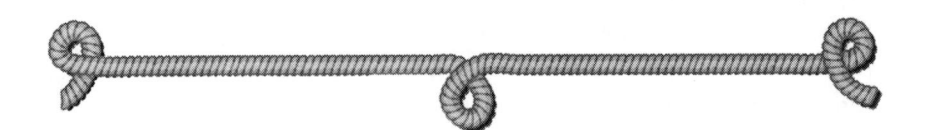

Day 38
"The Best Day Of My Life"

"The father of the righteous will greatly rejoice; he who fathers a wise son will be glad in him" (Proverbs 23:24 NIV).

    One day I had been at the TO ranch and then at our feed mill all day, and finally I decided that I should head home before dark. It's about an hour-and-fifteen-minute drive, so it lets me ponder about many things. The last week had been busy for us as we artificially inseminated heifers at both ranches amongst all the other normal day-to-day activities. I pondered about all the pasture movements that we needed to make before branding, as well as a million other things going through my mind. I thought about my family and wondered what they were doing and hoped I would get to play with my kids some before dark. I also pondered about my new obstacle in my fight with this insidious disease. Cara and I had been in Amarillo the prior Tuesday and Wednesday and found out that I had a five-centimeter tumor in my left heel bone. I had been limping for around a year, but I was limping on my other foot. The previous year I had surgery on my right foot to remove two bones that had cancer, and then I had 10 rounds of radiation treatment. The cancer in that foot was not totally gone, but it had been fairly stable for the prior few months. Then my "good foot" started hurting, and to be completely honest with you, I didn't want to know. I mean, seriously, that road was hard, and I really wanted to hide my head in the sand rather than find out. I had told my doctor that my foot hurt, but to get a bone metastasis in one foot is a 1/10,000 chance, and none of the docs had ever heard of metastasis to both feet. So, yes, to say the least my mind was full of thoughts as I drove home.

    It's always a good feeling to pull over the cattle guard to the ranch. Even though it's 10 miles from the house, it still feels like home. I love body condition scoring the cattle as I drive and studying the grass. As I looked to my right at one set of cows, I saw something that didn't seem right. There stood a yearling bull. I know that we hadn't placed bulls on the cows in that pasture, but we had put cover-up bulls on our heifers in the adjacent pasture. I called Zack and he had the bull numbers in front of him. Sure enough, 2557B was supposed to be in the Hacienda pasture. He obviously didn't want to wait for his heifers to re-cycle and decided that he would visit the cows next door. I looked at the digital clock on my pickup: 6:30 p.m. "I might have enough time to put him back in," I thought. I drove up to the barn and saw Cara and the kids horseback. Perfect. "I'll take them with me," I smiled. I booked it up to the house while Cara saddled my horse. Yes cowboys, I have the most wonderful wife in the world, but I also have an excuse. I was still in a walking boot and supposed to be on crutches, but I had hobbled around pretty good that afternoon. I undid my walking boot and tears filled my eyes as I slid my boot on. Nothing new, just a different foot. We drove out to where the cows were and I put out a little cake in a semi-circle and positioned the pickup and trailer so as to make a wing into the adjacent pasture. Getting from the driver's seat to the back of the trailer was not an easy task, but again, through tears of pain, I got it done. I shimmied up Casino (thank God and Silver Spur Ranches for that horse). I helped Grady on Sparky, and Josey and Cara mounted Barbie. I looked around and thought, "This is pretty cool." In about two minutes I had the bull separated from the cows and pushed through the gate, but then we really needed to drive him about a mile and a half to the water where we would find some heifers that he was supposed to be with. Grady is our cautious one, but I convinced him to go with me while Cara and Josey took the pickup around to meet us. For the next mile and a half he and I drove the bull back where he needed to go. Grady was 4, but you would have thought he was 14. He had ole Sparky's nose in Casino's tail the whole time. As far as ranch tasks go, it was pretty menial, but I think it was the greatest thing I have ever done on the Bell Ranch.

Zack was worried about me, I guess from my earlier call, and he texted me later that night to see if he needed to come the next morning. I told him that Grady and I got the bull. He replied, "Horseback???" I said, "Yes." He replied, "I bet that was fun." I texted, "The best day of my life." When I first found out about my other foot, I felt sorry for myself for about 48 hours. Then I decided that I was going to pull myself back up, point my nose to the wind and continue to live life to the fullest. And guess what? Every day since that day has also been the best day of my life.

Day 39
"Your Purpose"

"And we know that in all things God works for the good of those who love him, who have been called according to his purpose" (Romans 8:28 NIV).

I want to visit with you about something that had troubled me for a long time. It started when I first moved to Lubbock and started my graduate degree at Texas Tech. It was 2003 and Rick Warren's book, The Purpose Driven Live, had become really popular among Christian groups and churches. In fact, a large church on my way home was doing a church-wide study on the book. I had never really pondered what living a life with purpose was, but God put that seed in my mind in that season. A lot of other Christians were thinking about it as well, as Rick's book has sold over 30 million copies worldwide. I'm going to be honest, I've never read his book, but I'd like to share with you my journey to find my purpose in this life.

So, we have gone through the sequence in this devotional. We have gone through who we are, why we are and who we are going to be. We have learned that we are innately sinful, and when we finally decide to get over ourselves, we can decide whether or not to accept Jesus. If we do, however, then knowing Him is going to change us. Knowing Him is going to change our thought processes. Knowing Him is going to change the way we think about why we are here, why He created us at all.

Okay, I know exactly where some of you are. To you, your purpose in this life is to provide for your family. Your purpose is to work to earn things so that the ones around you can have a better life than you did. So, your purpose becomes your occupation. Your purpose is taking care of a set of cows, or making sure those stockers don't die. Maybe you aren't married and don't have kids. It's likely that your purpose is to better yourself through your occupation or social status. I get it, I really do. Making a living is a necessary and noble purpose. Yet, God designed every one of us for a unique purpose to serve His kingdom, and He gave us gifts and passions to use on said purpose.

"Wait, hold on," you say. "I'm not cut out to be Billy Graham." Fair enough. That's probably not your purpose then. "I am not cut out to be a missionary in Africa," you think. Me neither, and that's okay. Remember, God gave us unique gifts and passions. What we are to do is to use those gifts and passions to fulfill the purpose that He has put in our lives. Whatever your purpose is, it comes down to one central theme. Your purpose is to be a witness for Jesus Christ.

So, how do you get there from here? That was what perplexed me for so long. I knew that God had a calling or purpose for my life, but I had no idea what it was. I had led some Bible study groups, and had reached some lives, but I felt that He wanted me to do so much more. I also went through something that everyone will go through when searching their purpose. You must learn to overcome the fear of criticism to fulfill your purpose. Remember, God doesn't call the qualified; He qualifies the called. So, if He calls you to a purpose, He will make it happen. "What, then, shall we say in response to these things? If God is for us, who can be against us" (Romans 8:31 NIV)?

A couple years ago, I found my purpose. I started a Bible study ministry on Facebook called Western Faithbook. In less than two years our group has over 7,000 members. The reason that I know I can tell you that I have found my purpose is from the response of the people who follow my little blog. The life-changing stories and fervent prayer chains that have been started because of Western Faithbook have been incredible and at times overwhelming. My purpose is to be a witness for Jesus Christ, and in my mind if I can use my gifts, talents and passions to reach one soul, then my purpose is fulfilled. So, someday I may be able to hear Him say, "Well done, good and faithful servant! You have been faithful with a few things; I will put you in charge of many things. Come and share your master's happiness" (Matthew 25:21 NIV)! Cowboys, let me tell you one thing. Once you truly find a purpose for your life, all will be well with your soul.

Day 40
"I'll Drop You Off"

"I saw heaven standing open and there before me was a white horse, whose rider is called Faithful and True. With justice he judges and wages war. His eyes are like blazing fire, and on his head are many crowns. He has a name written on him that no one knows but he himself. He is dressed in a robe dipped in blood, and his name is the Word of God. The armies of heaven were following him, riding on white horses and dressed in fine linen, white and clean. Coming out of his mouth is a sharp sword with which to strike down the nations. "He will rule them with an iron scepter." He treads the winepress of the fury of the wrath of God Almighty. On his robe and on his thigh he has this name written: KING OF KINGS AND LORD OF LORDS" (Revelation 19:11-16 NIV).

It was well before sunrise. I caught one of new mounts that I had been assigned by the Matador Cattle Company. I was to be the headquarters man, and I surely didn't want anyone showing up to the saddle house without me first being saddled and ready to go. In fact, it was my first week, and although I had been around horses and cattle my entire life, I had never really worked for a big outfit with tradition and etiquette. Everyone had been gracious, however, and I was determined that I was going to learn quickly. Headquarters was essentially still Mick's country, and he would be leading the drive that morning. When everyone got ready, we jigged out south toward the Moore Pasture with the rising sun in a splendid panoramic to our east. After we trotted for about three miles, we entered the pasture in the northwest corner and Mick explained the drive. He was going to take most of the crew along the outside and swing the cows to the east. Another cowboy and I had to trot back to the west to kick out a neck of the pasture and then catch back up with the drive. I know it works differently in different country, but in the rolling plains of West Texas, the drive leader or the outside man is basically the boss. He is likely the wagon boss or camp man. He knows the country, knows where the cattle have been hanging and knows where they have tried you in the past. He sets the pace of the drive, and all the other men take their direction from him. Each man has his place on the drive, and it is a cardinal cowboy sin to get out of place or get in front of the boss.

I got lost that day in the Moore Pasture. We trotted back to the west just like he instructed, and I waited on my next man to come out, but I never saw him, so I hung back. By the time I realized that I was behind, it was too late and the drive had left me. A lot of cowboys have gotten lost on drives, but few will ever admit it. It's one of those things that you want to scrape from you mind with a chisel. So why am I telling you about it? A couple of reasons. First, I believe humility is one of the most powerful tools I have against myself, against my flesh. Once you figure that one out, you will be a lot further down the line. But the second reason is that I believe we have all been lost on the drive.

Cowboys, God is your drive leader. He sets the pace of your life and all men take their direction from Him. But along the way each of us has gotten lost. Each one of us had made some mistakes, and each one of us has a second chance. Verse 14 from the above scripture says, "The armies of heaven were following him, riding on white horses and dressed in fine linen, white and clean" (Revelation 19:14 NIV). That's us, gentlemen. That's the army of the Lord in the second coming of Christ in a battle to defeat Satan and evil once and for all. Can you imagine jigging in behind Christ for that drive?

Until then, "Take delight in the Lord and he will give you the desires of your heart" (Psalm 37:4 NIV). Learn who you are going to be in Christ, and find God's purpose for your life. Remember that things might get tough, but He will fight for you. Most importantly, on that fine day when His voice trumpets out, "I'll drop you off," have your horse saddled and ready to jig in behind your boss.

CPSIA information can be obtained at www.ICGtesting.com
Printed in the USA
LVOW10s1046110916

504133LV00022B/1022/P

9 781535 366137